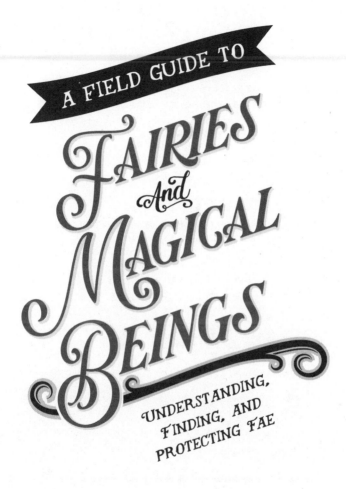

A FIELD GUIDE TO

Fairies *and* Magical Beings

UNDERSTANDING, FINDING, AND PROTECTING FAE

ILLUSTRATED BY KAYLEIGH EFIRD

CASTLE POINT BOOKS
NEW YORK

Compiled and edited from the following public domain texts:

Anderson, R. B. *Norse Mythology*. S. C. Griggs and Company, Chicago, 1876.

Campbell, John Gregorson. *Superstitions of the Highlands & Islands of Scotland.* James MacLehose and Sons, Glasgow, Scotland, 1900.

Sikes, Wirt. *British Goblins: Welsh Folk-lore, Fairy Mythology, Legends and Traditions*. George Bell & Sons, London, England, 1892.

Keightley, Thomas. *The Fairy Mythology: Illustrative of the Romance and Superstition of Various Countries*. Sampson Low, Marston, Searle, & Rivington, London, 1880.

www.castlepointbooks.com

Original fairy and magical creature art by Kayleigh Efird
Interior design by Melissa Gerber
Vintage and stock art used by permission from iStock.com and Shutterstock.com

The Castle Point Books trademark is owned by Castle Point Publishing, LLC.
Castle Point books are published and distributed by St. Martin's Publishing Group.

ISBN 978-1-250-37281-9 (trade paperback)
ISBN 978-1-250-37282-6 (ebook)

Our books may be purchased in bulk for promotional, educational, or business use. Please contact your local bookseller or the Macmillan Corporate and Premium Sales Department at 1-800-221-7945, extension 5442, or by email at MacmillanSpecialMarkets@macmillan.com.

First Edition: 2025

10 9 8 7 6 5 4 3 2 1

"Their quick feet pattered on the grass
As light as dewdrops fall.
I saw their shadows on the glass
And heard their voices call."

—Thomas Kennedy, "Night Dancers"

CONTENTS

CHAPTER 2:

A HISTORY OF FAIRY ENCOUNTERS 71

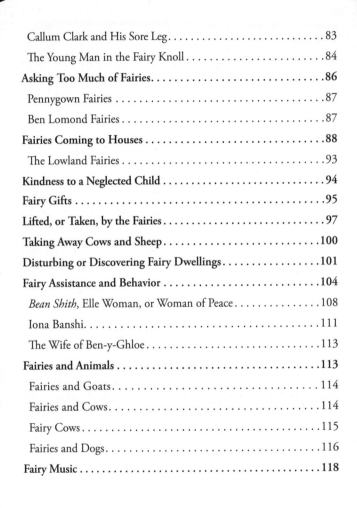

CHAPTER 3:
OTHER MAGICAL BEINGS *119*

INTRODUCTION

HUNDREDS OF YEARS AFTER FAIRY ENCOUNTERS WERE ROUTINELY DOCUMENTED ACROSS THE GLOBE, our instincts have been progressively dulled to the presence of magic. In the interest of simplicity, or perhaps because we are plagued by skepticism, we no longer trust the voice within that urges us to peer beyond the veil.

Thanks in great part to the unearthed nineteenth-century findings of John Gregorson Campbell, R. B. Anderson, Wirt Sikes, and Thomas Keightley and their careful documentation of all things fantastic, *A Field Guide to Fairies and Magical Beings* restores our ancient sense of wonder and offers useful time-tested information and oral histories on the mystical creatures that populate our homes, yards, forests, and towns. By lacing together an ancient tapestry of wisdom from Scotland, Ireland, England, Wales, and Scandinavia, with the added bonus of present-day tips and advice, rare and elusive beasts are yours to discover. Prepare to see the world with a heightened sense of awareness: Train your ears to the mischievous cackle of a pilfering Elf and the gentle flutter of a Pennygown Pixie's wings. Learn to differentiate a black rock from a Fairy spade and a pine needle from a Fairy arrow. With this valuable relic of antiquity to guide you, you will always know, for example, when a Fairy migration passes by on the eddy wind.

Not all magical beings, it should be mentioned, are to be loved and trusted like gentle pets. As a naturalist and explorer, it is crucial to know the danger that awaits in the wild. Heed the careful warnings of those who came before us when interacting with Fairies, Elves, Sprites, Trolls, Banshis, Changelings, Mermaids, Kelpies, and their enchanted brethren. These are not beings to be trifled with or teased. While some are generally faithful and friendly to curious and well-meaning humans, there are also plenty of menacing and evil beasts to avoid at all costs. This field guide is a valuable tool for pointing your attention and priming your senses to the mysteries, dangers, and unknowns of the supernatural realm.

*Never approach a mystical being without knowing exactly what kind it is. In general, it is best to abide by the simple rule, **live and let live**.*

Set out with an open mind and heart and revel in the act of exploring and discovering. Nature is resplendent with hidden miracles and curious beings that make life infinitely more intriguing. Use the patchwork of knowledge that follows, authentically preserved with the language and conventions of another place and time, to identify and preserve those wonders for generations to come.

CHAPTER 1

Fairies and Their Ways

In any account of Gaelic superstition and popular belief, the first and most prominent place is to be assigned to the Fairy or Elfin people, or, as they are called both in Irish and Scottish Gaelic, the *sìth* people, that is, "the people of peace," the "still folk," or "silently-moving" people. The antiquity of the belief is shown by its being found among all branches of the Celtic and Teutonic families, and in countries which have not, within historical times, had any communication with each other. If it be not entirely of Celtic origin, there can be no doubt that among the Celtic races it acquired an importance and influence accorded to it nowhere else. Of all the beings, with which fear or fancy peopled the supernatural, the Fairies were the most intimately associated with men's daily life. In the present day, when popular poetical ideas are extinguished in the universal call for "facts" and by "cold material laws," it is hard to understand how firm a hold a belief like this had upon men in a more primitive state of society, and how unwillingly it is surrendered.

Throughout the greater part of the Highlands of Scotland the Fairies have become things of the past. A common belief is that they existed once, though they are not now seen. There are others to whom the Elves* have still a real existence, and who are careful to take precautions against them. The changes, which the Highlands are undergoing, have made the traces of the belief fainter in some districts than in others, and in some there remains but a confused jumbling of all the superstitions. It would be difficult to find a person who knows the whole Fairy creed, but the tales of one district are never contradictory of those of another. They are rather to be taken as supplemental of each other.

---

*While Gaelic superstition groups Elves and Fairies together, Scandinavian legends offer further insight into the unique identity and personality of the Elf (see Chapter 3).

Fairy homes can be difficult to spot, especially since many Fairies make their dwellings underground. The most easy-to-spot Fairy home is the kind built into a hill or a mound of green earth or rock.

The Fairies, according to the Scoto-Celtic belief, are a race of beings, the counterparts of mankind in person, occupations, and pleasures, but unsubstantial and unreal, ordinarily invisible, noiseless in their motions, and having their dwellings underground, in hills and green mounds of rock or earth. They are addicted to visiting the haunts of men, sometimes to give assistance, but more frequently to take away the benefit of their goods and labours, and sometimes even their persons. They may be present in any company, though mortals do not see them. Their interference is never productive of good in the end, and may prove destructive. Men cannot therefore be sufficiently on their guard against them.

NAMES GIVEN TO FAIRIES

The names by which these dwellers underground are known are mostly derivative from the word *sìth* (pronounced *shee*). As a substantive (in which sense it is ordinarily used) *sìth* means "peace," and, as an adjective, is applied solely to objects of the supernatural world, particularly to the Fairies and whatever belongs to them. Sound is a natural adjunct of the motions of men, and its entire absence is unearthly, unnatural, not human. The name *sìth* without doubt refers to the "peace" or silence of Fairy motion, as contrasted with the stir and noise accompanying the movements and actions of men. The German "still folk" is a name of corresponding import. The Fairies come and go

with noiseless steps, and their thefts or abductions are done silently and unawares to men. The wayfarer resting beside a stream, on raising his eyes, sees the Fairy woman, unheard in her approach, standing on the opposite bank.

Fairies are stealthy creatures. It can be easier to see them than to hear them coming, since they seem to glide or walk on air.

Men know the Fairies have visited their houses only by the mysterious disappearance of the substance of their goods, or the sudden and unaccountable death of any of the inmates or of the cattle. Sometimes the Elves are seen entering the house, gliding silently round the room, and going out again as noiselessly as they entered. When driven away they do not go off with tramp and noise, and sounds of walking such as men make, or melt into thin air, as spirits

Fairy woman playing the flute.

do, but fly away noiselessly like birds or hunted deer. They seem to glide or float along rather than to walk. Hence the name *síth* and its synonyms are often applied contemptuously to a person who sneaks about or makes his approach without warning. Sometimes indeed the Elves make a rustling noise like that of a gust of wind, or a silk gown, or a sword drawn sharply through the air, and their coming and going has been even indicated by frightful and unearthly shrieks, a pattering as of a flock of sheep, or the louder trampling of a troop of horses. Generally, however, their presence is indicated at most by the cloud of dust raised by the eddy wind, or by some other curious natural phenomenon, by the illumination of their dwellings, the sound of their musical instruments, songs, or speech.

FAIRY-TRACKING TIP

When scouting for Fairies in nature,
listen for any of the following:

Rustling wind
Unearthly shriek
Galloping sound of feet or hooves
Instrumental music

For the same reason *sìth* is applied not merely to what is Fairy, but to whatever is Fairy-like, unearthly, not of this world. Of this laxer use of the term the following may be given as illustrations:

Breac shìth, "Elfin pox," hives, are spots that appear on the skin in certain diseases and indicate a highly malignant stage of the malady. They are not ascribed to the Fairies, but are called *sìth*, because they appear and again disappear as it were "silently," without obvious cause, and more mysteriously than other symptoms. Cows, said to have been found on the shores of Loscantire in Harris, Scorrybrec in Skye, and on the Island of Bernera, were called *cro sìth*, "Fairy cows," simply because they were of no mortal breed, but of a kind believed to live under the sea on *meillich*, seaweed. Animals in the shape of cats, but in reality witches or demons, were called *cait shìth*, "Elfin cats," and the Water-horse, which has no connection whatever with the Elves, is sometimes called *each sìth*, unearthly horse. The cuckoo is an *eun sìth*, a "Fairy bird," because, as is said, its winter dwelling is underground.

A banner in the possession of the family of Macleod, of Macleod of Skye, is called "Macleod's Fairy Banner" (*Bratach shìth MhicLèoid*), on account of the supernatural powers ascribed to it. When unfurled, victory in war (*buaidh chogaidh*) attends it, and it relieves its followers from imminent danger. Every pregnant woman who sees it is taken in premature labour (a misfortune which happened, it is said, to the English wife of a former chief in consequence of her irrepressible curiosity to see the banner), and every cow casts her calf (*cha bhi bean no bo nach tilg a laogh*). Others, however, say the name is owing to the magic banner having been got from an Elfin sweetheart.

A light, seen among the Hebrides, a sort of St. Elmo's light or Will-of-the-wisp, is called *teine sìth*, "Fairy light," though no one ever blamed the Fairies as the cause of it. In a semi-satirical song, of much merit for its spirit and ease of diction, composed in Tiree to the owner of a crazy skiff that had gone to the Ross of Mull for peats and stayed too long, the bard, in a spirited description of the owner's adventures and seamanship, says:

> "*Onward past Greenock,*
> *Like the deer of the cold high hills,*
> *Breasting the rugged ground*
> *With the hunter in pursuit;*
> *She sailed with Fairy motion,*
> *Bounding smoothly in her pride,*
> *Cleaving the green waves,*
> *And passing to windward of the rest.*"

This latitude in the use of the word has led some writers on the subject to confound with the Fairy beings having as little connection with them as with mankind. A similar laxness occurs in the use of the English word Fairy. It is made to include Kelpies, Mermaids, and other supernatural beings, having no connection with the true Fairy, or Elfin race.

FAIRY-TRACKING TIP

Indications that a Fairy is near:

A swirling cloud of dust
An illuminated mound of rock or earth
Items mysteriously disappearing

The following are the names by which the "folk" are known in Gaelic. It is observable that every one of the names, when applied to mortals, is contemptuous and disparaging.

Sithche (pronounced *sheeche*) is the generic and commonest term. It is a noun of common gender, and its plural is *sithchean* (sheechun). In Graham's *Highlands of Perthshire*, a work more than once quoted by Sir Walter Scott, but unreliable as an authority, this word is written *shi'ich*.

Sireach, plur. *sirich*, also *sibhrich*, is a provincial term; *an siriche du*, "the black Elf," *i.e.,* the veriest Elf.

Sithbheire (pronounced *sheevere*), a masculine noun, is mostly applied to Changelings, or the Elf substituted for children and animals taken by the Fairies. Applied to men it is very contemptuous.

Siochaire is still more so. Few expressions of scorn are more commonly applied to men than *siochaire grannda*, "ugly slink."

Duine sìth (plur. *daoine sìth*), "a man of peace, a noiselessly moving person, a Fairy, an Elf"; fem. *Bean shìth*, "a woman of peace, an Elle woman," are names that include the whole Fairy race. *Bean shìth* has become naturalized in English under the form *Banshi*. The term was introduced from Ireland, but there appears no reason to suppose the Irish belief different from that of the Scottish Highlands. Any seeming difference has arisen since the introduction of the Banshi to the literary world, and from the too-free exercise of imagination by book-writers on an imperfectly understood tradition.

The *leannan sìth*, "Fairy sweetheart, familiar spirit," might be of either sex. The use of this word by the translators of the Bible into Gaelic is made a great handle of by the common people, to prove from Scripture that Fairies actually exist. The Hebrew word so translated is rendered "pythons" by the Vulgate, and "consulters of the spirits of the dead" by modern scholars. Those said to have familiar spirits were probably a class of magicians, who pretended to be media of communication with the spirit world, their "familiar" making himself known by sounds muttered from the ground through the instrumentality, as the Hebrew name denotes, of a skin bottle.

Brughadair, "a person from a brugh, or Fairy dwelling," applied to men, means one who does a stupid or senseless action.

Other names are *sluagh*, "folk, a multitude"; *sluagh eutrom*, "light folk"; and *daoine beaga*, "little men," from the number and small size ascribed to the Elves.

Daoine Còire, "honest folk," had its origin in a desire to give no unnecessary offence. The "folk" might be listening, and were pleased when people spoke well of them, and angry when spoken of slightingly. In this respect they are very jealous. A wise man will not unnecessarily expose himself to their attacks, for, "Better is a hen's amity than its enmity" (*S'fhearr sìth ciree na h-aimhreit*). The same feeling made the Irish Celt call them *daoine matha*, "good people," and the lowland Scot "gude neighbours."

THE SIZE OF FAIRIES

The difference in size ascribed to the race, though one of the most remarkable features in the superstition, and lying on its surface, has been taken little notice of by writers. At one time the Elves are small enough to creep through keyholes, and a single potato is as much as one of them can carry; at another they resemble mankind, with whom they form alliances, and to whom they hire themselves as servants; while some are even said to be above the size of mortals, gigantic hags, in whose lap mortal women are mere infants.

In the Highlands the names *sìthche* and *daoine sìth* are given to all these different sizes alike, little men, Elfin youth, Elfin dame, and Elfin hag, all of whom are not mythical beings of different classes or kinds, but one and the same race, having the same characteristics and dress, living on the same food, staying in the same dwellings, associated in the same actions, and kept away by the same means. The easiest solution of the anomaly is that the Fairies had the power of making themselves large or small at pleasure. There is no popular tale, however, which represents them as exercising such a power, nor is it conformable to the rest of their characteristics that it should be ascribed to them.

The true belief is that the Fairies are a small race, the men "about four feet or so" in height, and the women in many cases not taller than a little girl (*cnapach caileig*). Being called "little," the exaggeration, which popular imagination loves, has diminished them till they appear as Elves of different kinds. There is hardly a limit to the popular exaggeration of personal peculiarities. Og, King of Bashan, was a big man, and the Rabbis made his head tower to the regions of perpetual snow, while his feet were parched in the deserts of Arabia. Finn MacCool was reputed strong, at least he thrashed the devil, and made him howl. A weaver in Perthshire, known as "the weaver with the nose" (*figheadair na eròine*), had a big nose, at least he carried his loom in it. Similarly the "little men" came down to the "size of half an ell," and even the height of a quart bottle.

The same peculiarity exists in the Teutonic belief. At times the Elf is a dwarfish being that enters through keyholes and window-slits; at other times a great tall man. In different localities the Fairies are known as Alfs, Huldra-Folk, Duergar, Trolls, Hill Folk, Little Folk, Still Folk, Pixies, etc. A difference of size, as well as of name, has led to these being described as separate beings, but they have all so much in common with the Celtic Fairies that we must conclude they were originally the same.

Legend has it that Elves and Fairies come in all sizes, though it's possible that they can change their size at will.

21

FAIRY DWELLINGS

The Gaelic, as might be expected, abounds in words denoting the diversified features of the scenery in a mountainous country. To this the English language itself bears witness, having adopted so many Gaelic words of the kind, as strath, glen, corrie, ben, knock, dun, etc. From this copiousness it arises that the round green eminences, which were said to be the residences of the Fairies, are known in Gaelic by several names which have no synonym in English.

Sìthein (pronounced shï-en) is the name of any place in which the Fairies take up their residence. It is known from the surrounding scenery by the peculiarly green appearance and rounded form. Sometimes in these respects it is very striking, being of so nearly conical a form, and covered with such rich verdure, that a second look is required to satisfy the observers it is not artificial. Its external appearance has led to its being also known by various other names.

Tolman is a small green knoll, or hummock, of earth; *bac*, a bank of sand or earth; *cnoc*, knock, Scot. "a knowe," and its diminutive *cnocan*, a little knowe; *dùn*, a rocky mound or heap, such, for instance, as the Castle Rock of Edinburgh or Dumbarton, though often neither so steep nor so large; *òthan*, a green elevation in wet ground; and *ùigh*, a provincial term of much the same import as tolman. Even lofty hills have been represented as tenanted by Fairies, and the highest point of a hill, having the rounded form, characteristic of Fairy dwellings is called its shï-en (*sìthein na beinne*). Rocks may be tenanted by the Elves, but not caves. The dwellings of the race are below the outside or superficies of the earth, and tales representing the contrary may be looked upon with suspicion as modern.

There is one genuine popular story in which the Fairy dwelling is in the middle of a green plain, without any elevation to mark its site beyond a horse skull, the eye sockets of which were used as the Fairy chimney.

These dwellings were tenanted sometimes by a single family only, more frequently by a whole community. The Elves were said to change their residences as men do, and, when they saw proper themselves, to remove to distant parts of the country and more desirable haunts. To them, on their arrival in their new home, are ascribed the words:

" Though good the haven we have left,
Better be the haven we have found."

The Fairy hillock might be passed by the strangers without suspicion of its being tenanted, and cattle were pastured on it unmolested by the "good people." There is, however, a common story in the Western Isles that a person was tethering his horse or cow for the night on a green *tolman* when a head appeared out of the ground, and told him to tether the beast somewhere else, as he let rain into "their" house, and had nearly driven the tether-pin into the ear of one of the inmates. Another, who was in the habit of pouring out dirty water at the door, was told by the Fairies to pour it elsewhere, as he was spoiling their furniture.

A Fairy with water leaking into its underground abode.

He shifted the door to the back of the house, and prospered ever after. The Fairies were very grateful to anyone who kept the sìthein clean, and swept away cow or horse droppings falling on it. Finding a farmer careful of the roof of their dwelling, keeping it clean, and not breaking the sward with tether-pin or spade, they showed their thankfulness by driving his horses and cattle to the sheltered side of the mound when the night proved stormy. Many believe the Fairies themselves swept the hillock every night, so that in the morning its surface was spotless.

Brugh (brŭ) denotes the Fairy dwelling viewed as it were from the inside—the interiors—but is often used interchangeably with *sìthein*. It is probably the same word as burgh, borough, or bro', and its reference is to the *number* of inmates in the Fairy dwelling.

FAIRY DRESSES

The Fairies, both Celtic and Teutonic, are dressed in green. In Skye, however, though Fairy women, as elsewhere, are always dressed in that colour, the men wear clothes of any colour like their human neighbours. They are frequently called *daoine beaga ruadh*, "little red men," from their clothes having the appearance of being dyed with the lichen called *crotal*, a common colour of men's clothes in the North Hebrides. The coats of Fairy women are shaggy, or ruffled (*caiteineach*), and their caps curiously fitted or wrinkled. The men are said, but not commonly, to have *blue* bonnets, and in the song to the murdered Elfin lover, the Elf is said to have a hat bearing "a smell of honied apples." This is perhaps the only Highland instance of a hat, which is a prominent object in the Teutonic superstition, being ascribed to the Fairies.

Fairies in their coats and wrinkled hats.

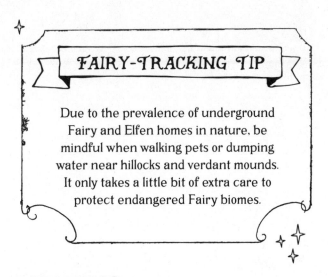

Due to the prevalence of underground
Fairy and Elfen homes in nature, be
mindful when walking pets or dumping
water near hillocks and verdant mounds.
It only takes a little bit of extra care to
protect endangered Fairy biomes.

FAIRY RINGS

The circles in the grass of green fields, which are commonly called
Fairy rings, are numerous in Wales, and it is deemed just as well to
keep out of them, even in our day. People no longer believe that the
Fairies can be seen dancing there, nor that the cap of invisibility will
fall on the head of one who enters the circle. They do believe that
the Fairies, in a time not long gone, made these circles with the tread
of their tripping feet, and that some misfortune will probably befall
any person intruding upon this forbidden ground. An elderly man at
Peterstone-super-Ely told me he well remembered in his childhood
being warned by his mother to keep away from the Fairy rings.

Signs of a Fairy ring under a canopy of oak trees.

FAIRY-TRACKING TIP

If you would like to see a real Fairy ring, your
best bet is to search under giant oak trees for
circular patterns in the grass. Be wary, however,
of stepping into the ring, because doing so
is said to bring misfortune to humans.

With regard to the Fairy rings, Jones held that the Bible alludes
to them, Matt. xii. 43. "The Fairies dance in circles in dry places; and
the Scripture saith that the walk of evil spirits is in dry places." They
favour the oak tree, and the female oak especially, partly because of its
more wide-spreading branches and deeper shade and partly because of
the "superstitious use made of it beyond other trees" in the days of the
Druids. Formerly, it was dangerous to cut down a female oak in a fair,
dry place. "Some were said to lose their lives by it, by a strange aching
pain which admitted of no remedy, as one of my ancestors did, but
now that men have more knowledge and faith, this effect follows not."

William Jenkins was for a long time the schoolmaster at Trefethin
Church in Monmouthshire, and, coming home late in the evening,
as he usually did, he often saw the Fairies under an oak within two
or three fields from the church. He saw them more often on Friday
evenings than any other. At one time, he went to examine the
ground about this oak, and there he found the reddish circle wherein
the Fairies danced, "such as have often been seen under the female
oak, called Brenhin-bren." They appeared more often to an uneven
number of persons, as one, three, five, etc., and more often to men
than to women.

Thomas William Edmund, of Hafodafel, "an honest pious man,
who often saw them," declared that they appeared, with one bigger
than the rest going before them in the company. They were also heard
talking together in a noisy, jabbering way, but no one could distinguish the words. They seemed, however, to be a very disputatious race,
insomuch, indeed, that there was a proverb in some parts of Wales to
this effect: *"Ni chytunant hwy mwy na Bendith eu Mamau"* (They will
no more agree than the Fairies).

FAIRY OCCUPATIONS

The Fairies, as has been already said, are counterparts of human-kind. There are children and old people among them; they practice all kinds of trades and handicrafts; they possess cattle, dogs, arms; they require food, clothing, sleep; they are liable to disease, and can be killed. So entire is the resemblance that they have even been betrayed into intoxication. People entering their brughs have found the inmates engaged in similar occupations to humans: spinning, weaving, grinding meal, baking, cooking, churning, sleeping, dancing, making merry, or sitting around a fire in the middle of the floor (as a Perthshire informant described it) "like tinkers." Sometimes they were absent on foraging expeditions or pleasure excursions. The women sing at their work, a common practice in former times with Highland women, and use the distaff, spindle, handmill, and other primitive implements. The men have smithies, in which they make the Fairy arrows and other weapons. Some Fairy families or communities are poorer than others, and they borrow meal and other articles of domestic use from each other and from their neighbours of mankind.

FAIRY FESTIVITIES

There are stated seasons of festivity that are observed with much splen-dour in the larger dwellings. The brugh is illumined, the tables glitter with gold and silver vessels, and the door is thrown open to all comers. Any of the human race entering on these occasions are hospitably and heartily welcomed; food and drink are offered them, and their health is pledged. Everything in the dwelling seems magnificent beyond description, and mortals are so enraptured that they forget everything but the enjoyment of the moment. Joining in the festivities, they lose all thought as to the passage of time. The food is the most sumptuous; the clothing the most gorgeous ever seen; the music the sweetest ever heard; the dance the sprightliest ever trod; the whole dwelling is lustrous with magic splendour.

Those who claim to have entered a Fairy brugh report warm hospitality from the Fae, including tables glistening with serving ware and alluring displays of endless food and drink.

All this magnificence and enjoyment, however, are nothing but a semblance and illusion of the senses. Humankind, with all their cares, toils, and sorrows, easily succumb to this more desirable state, and a person is greatly to be pitied whom the Elves get power over so that the person exchanges his or her human lot and labour for the Elves' society or pleasures. Wise people recommend that, in these circum-stances, a person should not utter a word until he comes out again, nor, on any account, should the person taste Fairy food or drink. If the person abstains from food and drink, he or she is very likely before long dismissed, but, if the person indulges, he or she straightaway loses the will and the power ever to return to human society. The person becomes insensible to the passage of time, and may stay, without knowing it, for years—even ages—in the brugh. Many who thus forgot themselves are still among the Fairies to this day. Should they ever again return to the open air, and their enchantment be broken, the Fairy grandeur and pleasure will prove an empty show, worthless, and fraught with danger. The food becomes disgusting refuse, and the pleasures a shocking waste of time.

FAIRY-TRACKING TIP

If you are ever lucky enough to be invited into a brugh during a Fairy celebration, politely refuse any food and drink. Stay too long, and you might lose your sense of time and all desire to leave.

The Fae are greatly adept at music and dancing, and a great part of their time seems to be spent in the practice of these accomplishments. The Changeling has often been detected by their fondness for these arts. Though in appearance an ill-conditioned and helpless brat, they have been known, when thinking they were unobserved, to play the pipes with surpassing skill and dance with superhuman activity. Elfin

The sound of a bagpipe could be a signal that an Elf or Fairy is nearby.

music is more melodious than that which human skill and instruments can produce, and there are many songs and tunes that are said to have been originally learned from the Fairies. The only musical instrument of the Elves is the bagpipes, and some of the most celebrated pipers in Scotland are said to have learned their music from them.

FAIRY RAIDS

The Gaelic belief recognises no Fairyland or realm different from the earth's surface on which people live and move. The dwellings are underground, but it is on the natural face of the earth where the Fairies find their sustenance, pasture their cattle, and forage and roam.

Their festivities are held on the last night of every quarter (*h-uile latha ceann ràidhe*), particularly the nights before Beltane (the first day of summer) and Hallowmas (the first of winter). On these nights, on Fridays, and on the last night of the year, they are given to leaving home and taking away whomsoever of the human race they find helpless, unguarded, or unwary. Fairies may be encountered any time, but on these stated occasions, humans are to be particularly on their guard against them.

On Fridays, they obtrusively enter houses and even have the impudence, it is said, to lift the lid off the pot to see what the family is cooking for dinner. Any Fairy story told on this day should be prefaced by saying, "A blessing attend their departing and travelling! This day is Friday, and they will not hear us" (*Beannachd nan siubhal 's nan isneachd! 'se 'n diugh Di-haoine 's cha chluinn iad sinn*). This prevents Fairy ill-will coming upon the storyteller for anything he or she may chance to say. No one should call the day by its proper name of Friday (*Di-haoine*) but should instead call it "the day of yonder town" (*latha bhatl' ud thall*). The Fairies do not like to hear the day mentioned, and if anyone is so unlucky as to use the proper name, the person can direct the Fairies' wrath elsewhere by adding "on the cattle of yonder town" (*air cro a bhail' ud thall*) or "on the farm of so-and-so," mentioning anyone he or she dislikes. The fear of Fairy wrath also prevents the sharpening of knives on Fridays.

FAIRY-TRACKING TIP

Fridays are adventurous days for Fairies, when they may be curious enough to venture into a home, so be on the lookout. If you notice that the lid has been removed from a pot you were cooking in or the oven door has been opened, there may be a hungry Fairy in your midst.

Fairies are said to come always from the west. They are admitted into houses, however well-guarded otherwise, in the following ways: by the little hand-made cake, the last of the baking (*bonnach beag boise*), called the *Fallaid* bannock, unless there has been a hole put through it with someone's finger, a piece broken off it, or a live coal put on the top of it; by the water in which people's feet have been washed, unless it is thrown out or has a burning peat put in it; by the fire, unless it is properly "raked" (*smàladh*), *i.e.,* covered up to keep it alive for the night; or by the band of the spinning wheel, if left stretched on the wheel. Unless the band was taken off the spinning wheel, particularly on Saturday evenings, the Fairies came after the residents of the house had retired to rest and used the wheel. Sounds of busy work were heard, but in the morning no work was found done, and possibly the wheel was disarranged.

A Fairy collecting water from a container generously left out by a human.

On the last night of the year, Fairies are kept out of the house by decorating the house with holly and dressing up the last handful of corn reaped as a Harvest Maiden (*Maighdean Bhuan*), then hanging it up in the farmer's house to aid in keeping them out until the next harvest.

CIRCUMSTANCES UNDER WHICH FAIRIES ARE SEEN

There seems to be no definite rule as to the circumstances under which the Fairies are to be seen. A person whose eye has been touched with Fairy water can see them whenever they are present; the seer, possessed of second sight, often sees them when others do not; and on nights on which the *shï-en* is open, the chance passerby sees them rejoicing in their underground dwellings. A favourite time for their encounters with people seems to be the dusk and wild stormy nights of mist and driving rain, when the streams are swollen and "the roar of the torrent is heard on the hill." They are also apt to appear when spoken of, when a desire is expressed for their assistance, when proper precautions are not taken and those whose weakness and helplessness call for watchfulness and care are neglected; when their power is scorned; and when a sordid and churlish spirit is entertained. Often, without fault or effort, in places the most unexpected, mortals have been startled by their appearance, cries, or music.

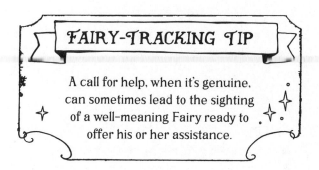

FAIRY FOOD

Fairy food consists principally of things intended for human food, of which the Elves take the *toradh, i.e.,* the substance, fruit, or benefit, leaving the semblance or appearance to humans. In this manner, they take cows, sheep, goats, meal, sowens (fermented oats), the produce of the land, etc. Cattle falling over rocks are particularly liable to being taken by them, and milk spilt in coming from the dairy is theirs by right. They have, of food peculiar to themselves and not acquired from humans, the root of silver weed (*brisgein*), the stalks of heather (*cuiseagan an fhraoich*), the milk of the red deer hinds and of goats, weeds gathered in the fields, and barleymeal. The *brisgein* is a root plentifully turned up by the plough in spring and ranked in olden times as the "seventh bread." Its inferior quality and its being found underground are probably the causes of its being assigned to the Fairies. As for the heather, it is a question whether the stalks are the tops or the stems of the plant; neither contain much sap or nourishment. The Banshi Fairy, or Elle woman, has been seen by hunters milking the hinds, just as people milk cows.

Preserving Fairies means protecting their natural resources. Whether that means opposing development in areas where red deer thrive or growing Fairy foods like heather, barley, and silverweed in your backyard, there are many ways to ensure that Fairies thrive in your area.

Those who partake of Fae food are as hungry after their repast as before it. In appearance, it is most sumptuous and inviting, but on grace being said turns out to be horse-dung. Some, in their haste to partake of the gorgeous viands, were only disenchanted when "returning thanks."

GIFTS BESTOWED BY FAIRIES

The Fairies can bestow almost any gift upon their favourites; they can give them great skill in music and in work of all kinds, give them cows and even children stolen for the purpose from others, leave them good fortune, keep cattle from wandering into their crops at night, assist them in spring and harvest work, etc. Sometimes their marvelous skill is communicated to mortals; sometimes they come in person to assist. If a smith, wright, or other tradesperson catches them working with the tools of his or her trade (a thing they are addicted to doing), Fairies can compel them to bestow on them the *Ceaird Chomuinn*, or association-craft, that is to come to their assistance whenever they want them. Work left near their hillocks overnight has been found finished in the morning, and they have been forced by people, entering their dwellings for this purpose, to reveal the cures for diseases defying human skill.

LOANS

"The giving and taking of loans," according to the proverb, "always prevailed in the world," and the custom is one to which the "good neighbours" are no strangers.

Fairies are universally represented as borrowing meal from each other and from humans. In the latter case, when they returned a loan, as they always honestly did, the return was in barleymeal, two measures for one of oatmeal; this, on being kept in a place by itself, proved inexhaustible, provided the bottom of the vessel in which it was stored was never made to appear, no question was asked, and no blessing was pronounced over it. It would then neither vanish nor become horse-dung!

When a loan is returned to them, they accept only the fair equivalent of what they have lent, neither less nor more. If more is offered, they take offence and never give an opportunity for the same insult again. We hear also of their borrowing a kettle or cauldron and, under the power of a rhyme uttered by the lender at the time of giving it, sending it back before morning.

EDDY WIND

When "the folk" leave home in companies, they travel in eddies of wind. In this climate, these eddies are among the most curious of natural phenomena. On calm summer days, they go past, whirling about straws and dust, and as not another breath of air is moving at the time, their cause is sufficiently puzzling. In Gaelic, the eddy is known as "the people's puff of wind" (*oiteag sluaigh*), and its motion "travelling on tall grass stems" (*falbh air chuiseagan treòrach*). By throwing one's left (or *toisgeul*) shoe at it, the Fairies are made to drop whatever they may be taking away—men, women, children, or animals. The same result is attained by throwing one's bonnet, saying, "this is yours; that's mine" (*Is leatsa so, is leamsa sin*); a naked knife; or earth from a mole-hill.

A whirl of straw and dust passing by on a calm day could be a community of Fairies.

Legend has it that people can be magically lifted in an eddy of Fairy wind.

In these strange Fairy eddies of wind, people going on a journey at night have been "lifted" and have spent the night careening through the skies. On returning to the earth, though they came to the same house they left, they were too stupefied to recognise either the house or its residents. Others, through Fairy spite, have wandered about all night on foot, failing to reach their intended destination though quite near it, and perhaps in the morning finding themselves on the top of a distant hill or in some inaccessible place to which they could never have made their way alone. Even in daylight, some were carried in the Elfin eddy from one island to another in great terror, lest they should fall into the sea.

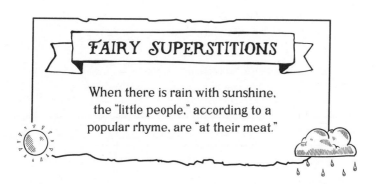

FAIRY SUPERSTITIONS

When there is rain with sunshine, the "little people," according to a popular rhyme, are "at their meat."

A calm day is perfect weather for Fairy tracking because it's easier to spot the out-of-place sight of an eddy wind. Look for a whirl of straw and dust if you want to see a group of Fairies in transit. Out of respect for their species, do not yield to the temptation of throwing your shoe at the eddy wind to watch the Fairies drop to the ground (as was once the custom).

FAIRY TOOLS

Natural objects of a curious appearance, or bearing a fanciful resemblance to articles used by humans, are also associated with the Fae. The reedmace plant is called the "distaff of the Fairy women" (a tool used for spinning yarn) and the foxglove the "thimble of the Fairy old women" (though more commonly the "thimble of dead old women"). A substance found on the shores of the Hebrides, like a stone, red (*ruadh*), half dark (*lith dhorcha*), and holed, is called "Elf's blood" (*fuil siochaire*). (In Northumberland, a fungous excrescence, growing about the roots of old trees, is called "Fairy butter.")

Reedmace (bulrush) and foxglove make handy tools for Fairies.

Depiction of a Fairy arrow (Figure 1. left) and a Fairy spade (Figure 1. right).
Variations of triangular flints (Figure 2) and healing spades (Figure 3).

45

The Fairy arrow (*Saighead shìth*) owes its name to a similar fancy. It is known also as "Fairy flint" (*spor shìth*) and consists of a triangular piece of flint, bearing the appearance of an arrowhead. It probably originally formed part of the rude armoury of the savages of the stone period. Popular imagination, struck by its curious form and ignorant of its origin, ascribed it to the Fairies. The Fairy arrow was said to be frequently shot at hunters, to whom the Elves have a special aversion because they kill the hinds, on the milk of which they live. They could not throw it themselves, but they compelled some mortal who was being carried about in their company to throw it for them. If the person aimed at was a friend, the thrower managed to miss the target, and the Fairy arrow proved innocuous. It was found lying beside the object of Fairy wrath and was kept as a valuable preservation against similar dangers in the future and for rubbing onto wounds. The person or beast struck by a Fairy arrow became paralyzed and, to all appearance, died shortly after. In reality, the afflicted was taken away by the Elves, and only their appearance remained. The arrow's point being blunt was an indication that it had done harm.

The Fairy spade is a smooth, slippery black stone, in shape "like the sole of a shoe." It was put in water and given to sick people and cattle.

CATTLE AND DEER

Everywhere in the Highlands, the red deer are associated with the Fairies and, in some districts, such as Lochaber and Mull, are said to be their only cattle. This association is sufficiently accounted for by the Fairy-like appearance and habits of the deer. In its native haunts, in remote and misty corries, where solitude has its most undisturbed abode, the deer's beauty and grace of form, combined with its dislike of the presence of people and even of the animals people have tamed, amply entitle it to the name of *sìth*. Timid and easily startled by every appearance and noise, a deer is said to be unmoved by the presence of the Fairies. Popular belief also says that no deer is found dead with age and that its horns, which it sheds every year, are not found, because they are hidden by the Fairies. In their transformations, it was peculiar for the Fairy women to assume the shape of the red deer; in that guise, they were often encountered by the hunters. The Elves have a particular dislike of those who kill the hinds and, on finding them in lonely places, delight in throwing elf-bolts at them. When a dead deer is carried home at night, the Fairies lay their weight on the bearer's back until the person feels as if he or she had a house for a burden. However, when a penknife is stuck in the deer, it becomes very light.

There are occasional allusions to the Fairy women having herds of deer. The Carlin Wife of the Spotted Hill (*Cailleach Beinne Bhric horò*), who, according to a popular rhyme, was "large and broad and tall," had a herd that she would not allow to descend to the beach and that "loved the water-cresses by the fountain high in the hills better than the black weeds of the shore." The old women of Ben-y-Ghloe, in Perthshire, and of Clibrich, in Sutherlandshire, seem to have been *sìth* women of the same sort. "I never," said an old man (he was upward of eighty years of age) in the Island of Mull, questioned some years ago on the subject, "heard of the Fairies having cows, but I always heard that deer were their cattle."

A deer sleeps peacefully as Fairies decorate its antlers.

In other parts of the Highlands, as in Skye, though the Fairies are said to keep company with the deer, they have cows like people have cows. When one of them appears among a herd of cattle, the whole fold of them grows frantic and starts lowing wildly. The strange animal disappears by entering a rock or knoll, and the others, unless intercepted, follow and are never more seen. The Fairy cow is dun (*odhar*) and "hummel," or hornless. In Skye, however, Fairy cattle are said to be speckled and red (*crodh breac ruadh*) and to be able to cross the sea. It is not on every place that they graze. There were not more than ten such spots in all of Skye. The field of Annat (*achadh na h-annaid*), in the Braes of Portree, is one. When the cattle came home at night from pasture, the following were the words used by the Fairy woman, standing on Dun Gerra-sheddar (*Dùn Ghearra-seadar*), near Portree, as she counted her charge:

"*Crooked one, dùn one,*
Little wing grizzled,
Black cow, white cow,
Little bull black-head,
My milch kine have come home,
O dear! that the herdsman would come!"

HORSES

In the Highland creed, the Fairies but rarely have horses. In Perthshire, they have been seen on a market day, riding about on white horses; in Tiree, two Fairy ladies were met riding on what seemed to be horses but in reality were ragweeds; and in Skye, the Elves have galloped the farm horses at full speed and in dangerous places, sitting with their faces to the tails.

When horses neigh at night, it is because they are ridden by the Fairies and pressed too hard. The neigh is one of distress, and if the hearer exclaims aloud, "Your saddle and pillion be upon you" (*Do shrathair's do phillein ort*), the Fairies tumble to the ground.

49

An adventurous Fairy dares to ride a horse.

FAIRY-TRACKING TIP

When tracking at night, it's wise to heed the superior instincts and heightened senses of nearby animals, who can perceive the presence of these magical creatures better than humans. A dog barking at an object unseen or a horse neighing insistently could indicate a mystical presence nearby.

DOGS

The Fairy dog (*cu sìth*) is as large as a two-year-old bull, dark green in colour, with ears of deep green. It is of a lighter colour toward the feet. In some cases, it has a long tail rolled up in a coil on its back, but others have the tail flat and plaited like the straw rug of a pack-saddle. Bran, the famous dog of Irish hero Finn MacCool, was of Elfin breed and, from the description given of it by popular tradition, decidedly parti-coloured:

> "Bran had yellow feet,
> Its two sides black and belly white;
> Green was the back of the hunting hound,
> Its two pointed ears blood-red."

Legend has it that there are mystical
Fairy hounds who act as Fairy watchdogs.

51

While a Fairy dog acts as a protector, regular dogs with no mystical origins tend to bark at and chase Fairies.

Bran had a venomous shoe (*Bròg nimhe*), with which it killed whatever living creature it struck. When at full speed and "like its father" (*dol ri athair*), it was seen as three dogs, intercepting the deer at three passes.

The Fairy hound was kept tied as a watchdog in the brugh but at times accompanied the Fairy women on their expeditions or roamed about alone, making its lairs in clefts of the rocks. Its motion was silent and gliding, and its bark a rude clamour (*blaodh*). It went in a straight line, and its bay was last heard, by those who listened for it, far out at sea. Its immense footprints, as large as the spread of the human hand, were found the next day, traced in the mud, in the snow, or on the sands. Others say it makes a noise like a horse galloping, and its bay is like that of another dog, only louder. There is a considerable interval between each bark, and at the third (it only barks thrice), the terror-struck hearer is overtaken and destroyed, unless he has by that time reached a place of safety.

Ordinary dogs have a mortal aversion to the Fairies and give chase whenever the Elves are sighted.

ELFIN CATS

Elfin cats (*cait shìth*) are explained to be of a wild, not a domesticated, breed. They are as large as dogs, of a black colour, and with a white spot on the breast, arched backs, and erect bristles (*crotach agus mùrlach*). Many maintain that these wild cats have no connection with the Fairies but are witches in disguise.

FAIRY THEFT

The Fae have earned a worse reputation for stealing than they deserve. So far as taking things without the knowledge or consent of the owners is concerned, the accusation is well-founded; they neither ask nor obtain leave, but there are important respects in which their depredations differ from the pilferings committed by criminals and other dishonest people.

The Fairies do not take their booty away bodily; they only take what is called in Gaelic its *toradh*, *i.e.,* its substance, virtue, fruit, or benefit. The outward appearance is left, but the reality is gone. Thus, when a cow is Elf-taken, it appears to its owner only as suddenly smitten by some strange disease. In reality, the cow is gone, and only its semblance remains, animated it may be by an Elf, who receives all the attentions paid to the sick cow but gives nothing in return. The seeming cow lies on its side and cannot be made to rise. It consumes the provender laid before it, but it does not yield milk or grow fat. In some cases, it gives plenty of milk, but milk that yields no butter. If taken up a hill and rolled down the incline, it disappears altogether. If it dies, its flesh ought not to be eaten—it is not beef but a stock of alder wood, an aged Elf, or some other substitute. Similarly, when the *toradh* of land is taken, there remains the appearance of a crop, but it is a crop without benefit to man or beast—the ears are unfilled, the grain is without weight, the fodder without nourishment.

A still more important point of difference is that the Fairies only take away what people deserve to lose. When mortals make a secret of, or grumble over, what they have, the Fairies get the benefit, and the owner is a poor person in the midst of abundance. When (to use an illustration the writer has more than once heard) a farmer speaks disparagingly of his crop and, though it be heavy, tries to conceal his good fortune, the Fairies take away the benefit of his increase. The advantage goes away mysteriously "in pins and needles," "in alum and madder," as the saying is, and the farmer gains nothing from the crop. Particularly articles of food, the possession of which people denied with oaths, became Fairy property.

A looting Fairy admires the articles she's hidden beneath a shrub.

The Elves are also blamed for taking with them articles mislaid. These are generally restored as mysteriously and unaccountably as they were taken away. A woman once blamed the Elves for taking her thimble. It was placed beside her but could not be found when she looked for it. Later, she was sitting alone on the hillside and found the thimble in her lap. This confirmed her belief in it being the Fairies that took it away. In a like mysterious manner, a person's bonnet might be whipped off his or her head or the pot for supper be lifted off the fire and left by invisible hands in the middle of the floor.

FAIRY-TRACKING TIP

Small objects that go missing and reappear may indicate that you should keep a close eye out for Fae. If an object goes missing, and you think the Fairy has taken a liking to it, consider leaving out similar objects and watching the area in the hopes of catching a Fairy red-handed.

The accusation of taking milk is unjust. It is brought against the Elves only in books, and never in the popular creed. The Fairies take cows, sheep, goats, and horses, which may give the substance or benefit (*toradh*) of butter and cheese, but not milk.

Many devices were employed to thwart Fairy inroads. A burning ember was put into sowens, one of the weakest and most unsubstantial articles of human food and very liable to Fairy attack. It was left there until the dish was ready for boiling, about three days after.

A sieve should not be allowed out of the house after dark, and no meal unless it be sprinkled with salt. Otherwise, the Fairies may, by means of them, take the substance out of all the farm's produce. For the same reason, a hole should be made with the finger in the little cake made with the remnant of the meal after a baking; when given to children, as it usually is, a piece should be broken off it. A nail driven into a cow, killed by falling over a precipice, was supposed by the more superstitious to keep the Elves away.

One of the most curious thefts ascribed to them was that of querns, or handmills. To keep them away, these handy and useful implements should be turned *deiseal, i.e.,* with a right-hand turn, as sunwise. What is curious in the belief is that it is said that people originally got the handmill from the Fairies themselves. Its sounds have often been heard by people as it was being worked inside some grassy knoll, and songs, sung by the Fairies employed at it, have been learned.

FAIRY SUPERSTITIONS

Some of the objects most frequently stolen (and replaced) by Fairies include:

Thimbles
Coins
Writing utensils
Buttons
Hats
Small kitchen items
Shoelaces
Cakes and sweets
Watches

CHANGELINGS

It is said that Fairies have the capacity to steal human children, though the reason is unclear, and few accounts of this exist in modern times. When they succeeded in their felonious attempts, legend states, the Elves left instead of the mother, and bearing her semblance, a stock of wood, and in place of the infant an old one of their own race. The Changeling child grew up a peevish misshapen brat, ever crying and complaining. It was known, however, to be a Changeling by the skillful in such matters, from the large quantities of water it drank—a tubful before morning, if left beside it—its large teeth, its inordinate appetite, its fondness for music and its powers of dancing, its unnatural precocity, or from some unguarded remark as to its own age. It is to the aged Elf, left in the place of child or beast, that the name *sith-bheire* (pronounced *"sheevere"*) is properly given. As may well be

A peevish and bratty Changeling (at left) appears similar to a human child (at right) to the untrained eye.

supposed, to call someone who has an ancient manner or look a sithb-heire, or to say the person "is only one who came from a brugh," is an expression of considerable contempt. When a person does a senseless action, it is said that the person has been "taken out of himself" (*air a thoirt as*), that is, taken away by the Fairies.

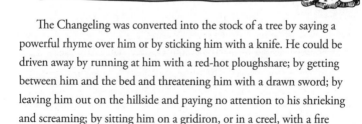

FAIRY SUPERSTITIONS

According to old legends, if you want to be sure to keep a mother and child safe from devious magical beings who might steal or hurt them, you can do the following:

Burn a shoe in a fire.

Write *keep out* in thread near the bed where mom and baby sleep.

Place something made of iron nearby.

Use quick wit!

The Changeling was converted into the stock of a tree by saying a powerful rhyme over him or by sticking him with a knife. He could be driven away by running at him with a red-hot ploughshare; by getting between him and the bed and threatening him with a drawn sword; by leaving him out on the hillside and paying no attention to his shrieking and screaming; by sitting him on a gridiron, or in a creel, with a fire below; by sprinkling him well out of the *maistir* tub; or by dropping him into the river. There can be no doubt these modes of treatment would rid a house of any disagreeable visitor, at least of the human race.

A Changeling in the nursery is a cause for alarm.

The story of the Changeling, who was detected by means of eggshells, seems in some form or other to be as widespread as the superstition itself. Empty eggshells are arranged around the hearth, and the Changeling, finding the house quiet and thinking to be alone, gets up from bed and examines them. Finding them empty, the Changeling is heard to remark sententiously, as he peers into each, "This is but a windbag; I am so many hundred years old, and I never saw the like of this."

NURSES

Fairies sometimes took care of children whom they found forgotten, and even of grown-up people sleeping incautiously in dangerous places.

The Elves also have children of their own, and they require the services of midwives like humans do. "Howdies," as they are called, taken in the way of their profession to the Fairy dwelling, found on coming out that the time they had stayed was incredibly longer or shorter than they imagined, and none of them was ever the better ultimately of her adventure.

THE MAN AND WOMAN OF PEACE

The Gaelic *sìthche*, like the English Elf, has two ideas, almost amounting to two meanings, attached to it. In the plural, *sìthchean*, it conveys the idea of a diminutive race, travelling in eddy winds, lifting people from the ground, stealing, and entering houses in companies; while in the singular, *sìthche*, the idea conveyed is that of one who approaches humankind in dimensions. The "man and woman of peace" hire themselves to the human race for a day's work or a term of service, and contract marriages with it. The Elfin youth has enormous strength, that of a dozen people, it is said, and the Elfin women (or Banshis) are remarkably handsome. The aged of the race were generally the reverse, in point of beauty.

MARRYING FAIRIES

Those who have taken Elfin women for wives have found a sad termination to their mésalliance. The defect or peculiarity of the fair enchantress, which her lover at first had treated as of no consequence, proves his ruin. Her voracity thins his herds, he gets tired of her or angry with her, and in an unguarded moment reproaches her with her origin. She disappears, taking with her the children and the fortune she brought him. The gorgeous palace, fit for the entertainment of kings, vanishes, and he finds himself again in his old black dilapidated hut, with a pool of rain-drippings from the roof in the middle of the floor.

THE *BEAN-NIGHE*, OR WASHING WOMAN

At times, the Fairy woman (*Bean shìth*) is seen in lonely places, beside a pool or stream, washing the linens of those soon to die, folding and beating them with her hands on a stone in the middle of the water. She is then known as the *Bean-nighe*, or washing woman, and her being seen is a sure sign that death is near.

In Skye, the Bean-nighe is said to be squat in figure, or not unlike a "small pitiful child". If a person caught her, she would tell that person all that would befall him or her in the afterlife. She would answer all of the person's questions, but the person must answer her questions, too. People did not like to reveal what she said to them.

If the person hearing the Bean-nighe at work, beating the clothes, caught her before being observed, then the washing woman could not hear the person. However, if the washing woman saw the person first, the person would lose the power of his or her limbs.

In the highlands of Perthshire, the washing woman is represented as small and round and dressed in pretty green. She spreads the linens by moonlight, winding the sheets of those soon to die. She can be caught by the person getting between her and the stream.

A Fairy washing woman hanging linens by moonlight.

She can also be caught and made to communicate her information at the point of the sword.

THE SONG OF THE FAIRY WOMAN

The song of the Fairy woman forebodes great calamity, and people do not like to hear it. Some describe it as "the fatal Banshi's boding scream," but it is not a scream, only a wailing murmur (*torman mulaid*) of unearthly sweetness and melancholy.

63

ELFIN QUEEN

The Banshi is, without doubt, the original Queen of Elfland, mentioned in ballads of the south of Scotland. The Elfin Queen met Thomas of Ercildoune by the Eildon tree and took him to her enchanted realm, where he was kept for seven years. In Gaelic, seven years is a common period of detention among the Fairies. She gave him the power of foretelling the future: "the tongue that never lied." At first, she was the most beautiful woman he had ever seen, but when he next looked, this is what he saw:

"The hair that hung upon her head,
The half was black, the half was grey,
And all the rich clothing was away
That he before saw in that stead;
Her eyes seemed out that were so grey,
And all her body like the lead."

The Fairy Queen.

The *leannan sìth,* "the Fairy who takes a human lover", communicates to her lover the knowledge of future events, and in the end she is looked upon by him with aversion. There is no mention, however, of Fairyland, or of an Elfin King or Queen, and but rarely of Fairies riding. True Thomas, who is as well known in Highland lore as he is in the Lowlands, is said to be still among the Fairies and to attend every market on the lookout for suitable horses. When he has made up his complement, he will appear again among men, and a great battle will be fought on the Clyde.

PROTECTION AGAINST FAIRIES

The great protection against the Elfin race (and this is perhaps the most noted point in the whole superstition) is *iron*, or preferably steel (*Cruaidh*). The metal, in any form—a sword, a knife, a pair of scissors, a needle, a nail, a ring, a bar, a piece of reaping-hook, a gun-barrel, a fish-hook (and tales abound that illustrate of all these)—is all-powerful.

On entering a Fairy dwelling, sticking a piece of steel, a knife, a needle, or a fish-hook in the door takes from the Elves the power of closing the door until the intruder comes out again. A knife stuck in a deer carried home at night keeps the Fairies from laying their weight on the animal. A knife or nail in one's pocket prevents the person from being "lifted" at night. Nails in the front bench of the bed keep Elves from women who have just given birth and their babes. As additional safeguards, the smoothing-iron should be put below the bed, and the reaping-hook in the window. A nail in the carcass of a bull that fell over a rock was believed to preserve its flesh from the Elves. Playing the mouth harp (*tromb*) kept the Elfin women at a distance from the hunter, because the tongue of the instrument is of steel. So also a shoemaker's awl in the doorpost of his bothy (cottage) kept a Glaistig from entering.

FAIRY-TRACKING TIP

Entering a Fairy dwelling is always a gamble, because time can pass more quickly in their world than ours. To make for an easier exit, it's wise to keep the door slightly ajar (preferably with a metal object to dull Fairy powers).

Fairies visiting a woman as she sleeps.

Fire thrown into water in which people's feet have been washed takes away the power of the water to admit the Fairies into the house at night; a burning peat put in sowens to hasten their fermenting kept the substance in them until ready to boil. Fire was carried around lying-in women and around children before they were christened, to keep mother and infant from the power of evil spirits. When the Fairies were seen coming in at the door, burning embers thrown toward them drove them away.

Another safeguard is *oatmeal*. When it is sprinkled on one's clothes or carried in the pocket, no Fairy will venture near, and it was usual for people going on journeys after nightfall to adopt the precaution of taking some with them. In Mull and Tiree, the pockets of boys going any distance after nightfall were filled with oatmeal by their anxious mothers, and old men are reminded to sprinkle themselves with it when going on a night journey.

In Skye, oatmeal was not looked upon as proper Fairy food, and it was said if people wanted to see the Fairies, they should not take oatmeal with them. If they did, they would not be able to see the Fairies.

Oatmeal, taken out of the house after dark, was sprinkled with salt; otherwise, the Fairies might, through its instrumentality, take the substance out of the farmer's whole grain. To keep them from getting the benefit of meal itself, people, when baking oatmeal bannocks, made a little thick cake with the last of the meal, between their palms (not kneading it like the rest of the bannocks), for the youngsters to put a hole through it with the forefinger. This palm bannock (*bonnach boise*) is not to be toasted on the gridiron but placed to the fire, leaning against a stone (*leac nam bonnach*), well known where a griddle is not available. The Fairies would be overtaken carrying with them the benefit (*toradh*) of the farm in a large thick cake, with the handle of the quern (*sgonnan na brà*) stuck through it and forming a pole on which it was carried. This cannot occur when the last bannock baked (*Bonnach fallaid*) is a little cake with a hole in it (*Bonnach beag's toll ann*).

FAIRY SUPERSTITIONS

Maistir, or stale urine, kept for the scouring of blankets and other cloth, when sprinkled on the cattle and on the doorposts and walls of the house, kept the Fairies, and indeed every mischief, at a distance. This sprinkling was done regularly on the last evening of every quarter of the year (*h-uile latha ceann ràidhe*).

Plants of great power were the *Mòthan* (*Sagina procumbens*, trailing pearlwort) and *Achlasan Challum-chille* (*Hypericum pulcrum*, St. John's wort). The former protected its possessor from fire and the attacks of the Fae. The latter warded off fevers and kept the Fairies from taking people away in their sleep. There are rhymes that must be said when these plants are pulled.

Stories representing the Bible as a protection must be of a recent date. It is not so long since a copy of the Bible was not available in the Highlands for that or any other purpose. When the book did become accessible, it is not surprising that, as in other places, reverence should accumulate around it.

NOTABLE FAIRY CHARACTERISTICS

Such are the main features of the superstition of the *sìthchean*, the still-folk, the noiseless people, as it existed, and in some degree still exists, in the Highlands and particularly in the islands of Scotland. There is a clear line of demarcation between it and every other Highland superstition, though the distinction has not always been observed by writers on the subject. The following Fairy characteristics deserve to be particularly noticed.

It was peculiar to the Fairy women to assume the shape of *deer*, while witches became mice, hares, cats, gulls, or black sheep, and the devil a he-goat or gentleman with a horse's or pig's foot.

A running stream could not be crossed by evil spirits, ghosts, and apparitions, but made no difference to the Fairies. If all tales be true, they could give a dip in the passing to those they were carrying away, and the stone, on which the washing woman folded the linens of the doomed, was in the middle of water.

Witches took the milk from cows, but the Fairies had cattle of their own. When Fairies attacked the farmer's dairy, it was to take away the cows themselves, after which the cow in appearance remained, but its benefit (the real cow) was gone. The Elves have even the impertinence at times to drive back the cow at night to pasture on the corn of the person from whom they have stolen it.

The frenzy with which Fairy women afflicted human men was a wandering madness, which made them roam about restlessly, without knowing what they were doing, or leave home at night to hold appointments with the Elfin women themselves. By Druidism, men were driven from their kindred and made to imagine themselves undergoing marvelous adventures and changing shape.

Dogs crouched or leapt at their master's throat in the presence of evil spirits, but they gave chase to the Fae.

Night alone was frequented by the powers of darkness, and they fled at the cock-crowing; however, the Fairies were encountered in the daytime as well.

FAIRY-TRACKING TIP

Clear your pockets of coins and keys and remove jewelry and belt buckles to increase the chances of a successful Fairy-finding mission. Legend has it that metals, especially iron and steel, in any form limit the Fairies' powers and keep them away.

CHAPTER 2

A History of Fairy Encounters

At eve, the primrose path along,
The milkmaid shortens with a song
Her solitary way;
She sees the Fairies with their queen
Trip hand-in-hand the circled green,
And hears them raise, at times unseen,
The ear-enchanting lay.

—Rev. John Logan, Ode to Spring, 1780

There be few among us who have not felt evanescent regrets for the displacement by the old faith in Fairies. There was something so peculiarly fascinating in that old belief that, "once upon a time," the world was less practical in its facts than now, less commonplace and humdrum, less subject to the inexorable laws of gravity, optics, and the like. What dramas it has yielded! What poems, what dreams, what delights!

But since the knowledge of our maturer years threatens to destroy all that, it is a comfort to lovers of Fairy legends to find that they need not sweep them into the grate as so much rubbish; on the contrary, they become even more enchanting in the crucible of science than they were in their old character.

WHY THESE STORIES MATTER TODAY

The diverse legends to follow offer modern-day
Fairy trackers and conservationists a deeper
sense of the winged and wondrous Fae who have
captured our curiosity and inspired us to seek
them out. Whether they are positive encounters
or cautionary tales of sightings gone awry, the
details of these legends offer clues to guide us as
we venture boldly into the wild. In reading these
captivating tales, we also join hearts and minds with
previous generations of believers. If we are lucky
enough to witness magical beings in our homes or
our backyards or our forest groves, let us put pen to
paper and add to this rich archive of Fairy legends.

TALES OF THOSE WHO HAVE ENTERED FAIRY DWELLINGS

The few brave humans who venture boldly, or accidentally, into a Fairy
brugh should be ready for anything to happen. If they play their hand
well, they may be healed or gifted with abilities. But if they rub their
mystical hosts the wrong way, or meet a more sinister breed of Fairy,
serious consequences may befall them.

The Welsh Tale of Tudur of Llangollen

It will help you to know, dear reader, that the Welsh Fairies seek to entice mortals to dance with them, and when anyone is drawn to do so, it is more than probable that the person will not return for a long time. The scene of this tale is a hollow near Llangollen, on the mountainside halfway up to the ruins of Dinas Bran Castle, which to this day is called Nant yr Ellyllon. It obtained its name, according to tradition, in this way:

A young man, called Tudur ap Einion Gloff, used to, in old times, pasture his master's sheep in that hollow. One summer's night, when Tudur was preparing to return to the lowlands with his woolly charge, there suddenly appeared, perched upon a stone near him, "a little man in moss breeches with a fiddle under his arm." He was the tiniest wee specimen of humanity imaginable. His coat was made of birch leaves, and he wore upon his head a helmet consisting of a gorse flower, while his feet were encased in pumps made of beetle's wings. He ran his fingers over his instrument, and the music made Tudur's hair stand on end.

"*Nos da'ch', nos da'ch'*," said the little man, which means "Goodnight, goodnight to you," in English.

"*Ac i chwithau*," replied Tudur; which, in English, means "The same to you." Then continued the little man, "You are fond of dancing, Tudur, and if you but tarry awhile, you shall behold some of the best dancers in Wales, and I am the musician."

Quoth Tudur, "Then where is your harp? A Welshman even cannot dance without a harp."

"Oh," said the little man, "I can discourse better dance music upon my fiddle."

"Is it a fiddle you call that stringed wooden spoon in your hand?"

Fairies with an eye for fashion have been said to craft beautiful hats from tulips, gorse flowers, and bellflowers.

asked Tudur, for he had never seen such an instrument before. And now Tudur beheld through the dusk hundreds of pretty little Sprites converging toward the spot where they stood, from all parts of the mountain. Some were dressed in white, and some in blue, and some in pink, and some carried glow-worms in their hands for torches. And so lightly did they tread that not a blade nor a flower was crushed beneath their weight. Everyone made a curtsy or a bow to Tudur as they passed, and Tudur doffed his cap and moved to them in return. Presently, the little minstrel drew his bow across the strings of his instrument, and the music produced was so enchanting that Tudur stood transfixed to the spot. At the sound of the sweet melody, the Tylwyth Teg arranged themselves in groups and began to dance.

Now of all the dancing Tudur had ever seen, none was to be compared to that he saw going on at that moment. He could not help keeping time with his hands and feet to the merry music, but he dared not join in the dance, "for he thought within himself that to dance on a mountain at night in strange company, to perhaps the devil's fiddle, might not be the most direct route to heaven." But at last he found there was no resisting this bewitching strain, joined to the sight of the capering Ellyllon.

"Now for it, then," screamed Tudur, as he pitched his cap into the air under the excitement of delight. "Play away, old devil; brimstone and water, if you like!"

No sooner were the words uttered than everything underwent a change. The gorse-blossom cap vanished from the minstrel's head, and a pair of goat's horns branched out instead. His face turned as black as soot and a long tail grew out of his leafy coat, while cloven feet replaced the beetle-wing pumps.

Tudur's heart was heavy, but his heels were light. Horror was in his bosom, but the impetus of motion was in his feet. The Fairies changed into a variety of forms. Some became goats, and some became dogs; some assumed the shape of foxes, and others that of cats. It was the strangest crew that ever surrounded a human being. The dance became at last so furious that Tudur could not distinctly make out the forms of the dancers. They reeled around him with such rapidity that they almost resembled a wheel of fire. Still, Tudur danced on. He could not stop; the devil's fiddle was too much for him, as the figure with the goat's horns kept pouring it out with unceasing vigour, and Tudur kept reeling around in spite of himself.

The next day, Tudur's master ascended the mountain in search of the lost shepherd and his sheep. He found the sheep all right at the foot of the Fron, but fancy his astonishment when, ascending higher, he saw Tudur spinning like mad in the middle of the basin now known as Nant yr Ellyllon. Some pious words of the master broke the charm and restored Tudur to his home in Llangollen, where he told his adventures with great gusto for many years afterward.

Fairies dancing in a circle.

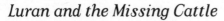

Luran and the Missing Cattle

This is a tale, diffused in different forms, over the whole West Highlands. Versions of it have been heard from Skye, Ardnamurchan, Lochaber, Craignish, Mull, and Tiree, differing only slightly from each other.

The Charmed Hill (*Beinn Shianta*), from its height, greenness, or pointed summit, forms a conspicuous object on the Ardnamurchan coast, at the north entrance of the Sound of Mull. On the "shoulder" of this hill, were two hamlets, Sgìnid and Corryvulin, the lands attached to which, now forming part of a large sheep farm, were at one time occupied in common by three tenants, one of whom was named Luran Black (*Luran Mac-ille-dhui*).

One particular season, a cow of Luran's was found unaccountably dead each morning. Suspicion fell on the tenants of the culver (*an cuilibheir*), a green knoll in Corryvulin, having the reputation of being tenanted by the Fairies. Luran resolved to watch his cattle for a night and ascertain the cause of his mysterious losses. Before long, he saw the culver opening and a host of little people pouring out. They surrounded a grey cow (*mart glas*) belonging to him and drove it into the knoll. Not one busied himself in doing this more than Luran himself; he was, according to the Gaelic expression, "as one and as two" (*mar a h-aon 's mar a dhà*) in his exertions.

The cow was killed and skinned. An old Elf, a tailor sitting in the upper part of the brugh, with a needle in the right lapel of his coat, was forcibly caught hold of, stuffed into the cow's hide, and sewn up. He was then taken to the door and rolled down the slope. Festivities commenced, and whoever might be on the floor dancing, Luran was sure to be. He was "as one and as two" at the dance, as he had been at driving the cow. A number of gorgeous cups and dishes were put on the table, and Luran, resolving to make up for the loss of the grey cow, watched his opportunity and made off with one of the cups (*còrn*). The Fairies observed him and started in pursuit. He heard one of them remark, "Not swift would be Luran, if it were not the hardness of his bread."

Luran's Fairy encounter began with a stolen cow.

His pursuers were likely to overtake him when a friendly voice called out, "Luran, Luran Black, betake thee to the black stones of the shore." Below the high-water mark, no Fairy, ghost, or demon can come, and, acting on the friendly advice, Luran reached the shore and, keeping below the tide mark, made his way home in safety. He heard the outcries of the person who had called out to him (probably a former acquaintance who had been taken by "the people"), who was now being belaboured by the Fairies for his ill-timed officiousness.

The next morning, the grey cow was found lying dead, with its feet in the air, at the foot of the Culver, and Luran said that a needle would be found in its right shoulder. On this proving to be the case, he allowed none of the flesh to be eaten and threw it out of the house.

One of the fields, tilled in common by Luran and two neighbours, was every year, when ripe, reaped by the Fae in one night, and the benefit of the crop disappeared. An old man was consulted, and he undertook to watch the crop. He saw the shï-en of Corryvulin open and a troop of people coming out. There was an old man at their head, who put the company in order: some to shear, some to bind the sheaves, and some to make stooks. On his word, the field was reaped in a wonderfully short time. The watcher, calling aloud, counted the reapers. The Fairies never troubled the field again.

Their persecution of Luran did not, however, cease. While on his way to Inveraray Castle, with his Fairy cup, he was lifted mysteriously with his treasure out of the boat in which he was taking his passage and was never seen or heard of after.

According to another Ardnamurchan version, Luran was a butler boy in Mingarry Castle. One night, he entered a Fairy dwelling and found the company within feasting and making merry. A shining cup, called *an cupa cearrarach*, was produced, and whatever liquor the person holding the cup wished for would appear in the cup. Whenever a dainty appeared on the table, Luran was asked, "Did you ever see the like of that in Mingarry Castle?"

At last, the butler boy wished the cup to be full of water, and, throwing its contents on the lights and extinguishing them, he ran away with the cup in his hand. The Fairies gave chase. Someone among them called out to Luran to make for the shore. He reached the friendly shelter and made his way below the high-water mark to the castle, which he entered by a stair leading to the sea. The cup remained long in Mingarry Castle, but it was at last lost in a boat that sank at Mail Point (*Rutha Mhàil*).

The Cup of the Macleods of Raasa

The magical cups of Fairies are said to be replenished with any item you wish.

In Raasa, a man, named Hugh, entered a Fairy dwelling where there was feasting going on. The Fairies welcomed him heartily and pledged his health. "Here's to you, Hugh," and "I drink to you, Hugh" (*cleoch ort, Eoghain*), was to be heard on every side. He was offered drink in a fine glittering cup. When he got the cup in his hands, he ran off with it. The Fairies let loose one of their dogs after him. He made his escape and heard the Fairies calling back the dog by its name, Farvann (*Farbhann! Farbhann!*). The cup long remained in the possession of the Macleods of Raasa.

The Fairies on Finlay's Sandbank

The sandbank of this name (*Bac Fhionnlaidh*) on the farm of Ballevulin, in Tiree, was at one time a noted Fairy residence, but it has since been blown level with the ground. It caused surprise to many that no traces of the Fae were found in it. Its Fairy tenants were at one time in the habit of sending every evening to the house of a smith in the neighbourhood for the loan of a kettle (*iasad coire*). The smith, when giving it, always said:

"A smith's due is coals,
And to send cold iron out;
A cauldron's due is a bone,
And to come safe back."

Under the power of this rhyme, the cauldron was restored safely before morning. One evening, the smith was away from home, and his wife, when the Fairies came for the usual loan, never thought of saying the rhyme. In consequence, the cauldron was not returned. On finding this out, the smith scolded his wife. She, irritated by his reproaches, rushed away for the kettle. She found the brugh open, went in, and (as is recommended in such cases), without saying a word, snatched up the cauldron and made off with it. When going out at the door, she heard one of the Fairies calling out:

Making deals with Fairies, or loaning them items, always comes with some risk.

> *"Thou dumb sharp one, thou dumb sharp,*
> *That came from the land of the dead,*
> *And drove the cauldron from the brugh—*
> *Undo the Knot, and loose the Rough."*

She succeeded in getting home before Rough, the Fairy dog, overtook her, and the Fairies never again came for the loan of the kettle.

Callum Clark and His Sore Leg

Some six generations ago, there lived at Port Vista (*Port Bhissta*) in Tiree a dark, fierce man, known as Big Malcolm Clark (*Callum mòr mac-a-Chleirich*). He was a very strong man and, in his brutal violence, produced the death of several people. Tradition also says of him that he killed a Water-horse and fought a Banshi with a horse-rib at the long hollow, covered in winter with water, called the *Léig*. In this encounter, his own little finger was broken.

When sharpening knives, old women in Tiree said, "Friday in Clark's town" (*Di-haoine am baile mhic-a-Chleirich*), with the intent of making him the object of Fairy wrath. One evening, as he was driving a tether-pin into a hillock, a head popped up out of the ground and told him to find some other place for

Fairies are said to be experts in the healing powers of nature.

83

securing his beast, as he was letting the rain into their dwelling.

Sometime after this, he had a painfully sore leg (*bha i gu dòruin-neach doirbh*). He went to the shï-en, where the head had appeared, and, finding it open, entered in search of a cure for his leg. The Fairies told him to put "earth on the earth" (*Cuir an talamh air an talamh*). He applied every kind of earth he could think of to the leg, but without effect. At the end of three months, he went again to the hillock and, when entering, put steel (*cruaidh*) in the door. He was told to go out, but he would not, nor would he withdraw the steel until he was told the proper remedy. At last, he was told to apply the red clay of a small loch in the neighbourhood (*criadh ruadh Lochan ni'h fhonhairle*). He did so, and the leg was cured.

The Young Man in the Fairy Knoll

Two young men, coming home after nightfall on Halloween, each with a jar of whisky on his back, heard music by the roadside and, seeing a dwelling open and illuminated, and dancing and merriment going on within, entered. One of them joined the dancers, without as much as waiting to lay down the burden he was carrying. The other, suspecting the place and company, stuck a needle in the door as he entered, and got away when he liked. On that day, one year later, he came back for his companion and found him still dancing with the jar of whisky on his back. Though more than half-dead with fatigue, the enchanted dancer begged to be allowed to finish the reel. When brought to the open air, he was only skin and bone.

This tale is localised in the Ferintosh district and at the Slope of Big Stones (*Leathad nan Clacha mòra*) in Harris. In Argyllshire, people say it happened in the north. In the Ferintosh story, only one of the young men entered the brugh, and the door immediately closed. The other lay under suspicion of having murdered his companion, but, by advice of an old man, he went to the same place on the same night the following year and, by putting steel in the door of the Fairy dwelling, which he found open, recovered his companion.

When entering a Fairy dwelling, it is safest to put a needle or fish-hook in the doorjamb in case a quick exit is needed.

It is well known that Highland Fairies, who speak English, are the most dangerous of any. A young man was sent for the loan of a sieve and, mistaking his way, entered a brugh, which was open that evening. He found there two women grinding at a handmill, two women baking, and a mixed party dancing on the floor. He was invited to sit down: "Farquhar MacNeill, be seated" (*Fhearchair 'ie Neill, bi 'd shuidhe*). He thought he would first have a reel with the dancers. He forgot all about the sieve and lost all desire to leave the company he was in.

One night, he accompanied the band among whom he had fallen on one of its expeditions and, after careening through the skies, got stuck in the roof of a house. Looking down the chimney (*fàr-leus*), he saw a woman bouncing a child on her knee and, struck with the sight, exclaimed, "God bless you" (*Dia gu d'bheannachadh*). When he pronounced the Holy Name, he was disenchanted and tumbled down the chimney! On coming to himself, he went in search of his relatives. No one could tell him anything about them.

At last, he saw, thatching a house, an old man so grey and thin that he took him for a patch of mist resting on the housetop. He went and made inquiries of him. The old man knew nothing of the parties asked for, but said perhaps his father did. Amazed, the young man asked him if his father was alive, and on being told he was and where to find him, he entered the house. He there found a very venerable man sitting in a chair by the fire, twisting a straw-rope for the thatching of the house (*snìomh sìomain*). This man also, on being questioned, said he knew nothing of the people, but perhaps his father did. The father he referred to was lying in bed, a little shrunken man, and he in like manner referred to his father. This remote ancestor, being too weak to stand, was found in a purse (*sporran*) suspended at the end of the bed. On being taken out and questioned, the wizened creature said, "I did not know the people myself, but I often heard my father speaking of them." On hearing this, the young man crumbled in pieces and fell down a bundle of bones (*cual chnàmh*).

ASKING TOO MUCH OF FAIRIES

There are many stories of well-meaning Fairies who, when presented with materials and a clear task, will gift humans with their handiwork and craft items to completion. However, if humans seem thankless or press their goodwill too far, their requests go unheeded.

Pennygown Fairies

A green mound, near the village of Pennygown (*Peigh'nn-a-ghobhann*), in the parish of Salen, Mull, was at one time occupied by a benevolent company of Fairies. People had only to leave at night on the hillock the materials for any work they wanted done, such as wool to be spun, thread for weaving, etc., and tell what was wanted, and before morning the work was finished. One night, someone left the wood of a fishing-net buoy and a short, thick piece of wood, with a request to have it made into a ship's mast. The Fairies were heard toiling all night and singing, "Short life and ill luck attend the man who asked us to make a long ship's big mast from the wood of a fishing-net buoy." In the morning, the work was not done, and these Fairies never after did anything for anyone.

Ben Lomond Fairies

A company of Fairies lived near the Green Loch (*Lochan Uaine*) on Ben Lomond. Whatever was left overnight near the loch—cloth, wool, or thread—was dyed by them in any desired colour before morning. A specimen of the desired colour had to be left at the same time. A person left a quantity of undyed thread and a piece of black and white twisted thread along with it, to show that he wanted part of the hank black and part white. The Fairies thought the pattern was to be followed, and the work done at the same time as the dyeing. Not being able to do this, they never dyed any more.

FAIRIES COMING TO HOUSES

Ewen, son of Allister Og, was a shepherd in the Dell of Banks (*Coira Bhaeaidh*), at the south end of Loch Ericht (*Loch Eireachd*), and stayed alone in a bothy (shelter) far away from other houses. In the evenings, he put the porridge for his supper out to cool on top of the double wall (*anainn*) of the hut. On successive evenings, he found it pitted and pecked all around the edges, as if by little birds or heavy rain-drops. He watched, and he saw little people coming and pecking at his porridge. He made little dishes and spoons of wood and left them beside his own dish. The Fairies, understanding his meaning, took to using these and let the big dish alone. At last, they became quite familiar with Ewen, entered the hut, and stayed whole evenings with him. One evening, a woman came with them. There was no dish for her, and she sat on the other side of the house, saying never a word, but grinning and making faces at the shepherd whenever he looked her way. Ewen at last asked her, "Are you always like that, my lively maid?" Owing to the absurdity of the question, or Ewen's failure to understand that the grinning was a hint for food, the Fairies never came again.

The Elves came to a house at night and, finding it closed, called upon "Feet-water," *i.e.*, water in which people's feet had been washed, to come and open the door. The water answered from somewhere nearby that it could not, as it had been poured out. They called on the Band of the Spinning Wheel to open the door, but it answered that it could not, as it had been thrown off the wheel. They called upon Little Cake, but it could not move, as there was a hole through it and a live coal on the top of it. They called upon

Fairies eating porridge and fruit.

Fairies are said to enter homes through an open keyhole.

the "raking" coal, but the fire had been secured in a proper manner to keep it alive all night. This is a tale not localised anywhere, but universally known.

A man observed a band of people dressed in green coming toward the house, and, recognising them to be Fairies, ran in great terror, shut and barred the door, and hid himself below the bed. The Fairies, however, came through the keyhole and danced on the floor, singing. The song extended to several verses, to the effect that no kind of house could keep out the Fairies, not a turf house nor a stone house.

The Fairies staying in Dunruilg came to assist a farmer in the vicinity in weaving and preparing cloth and, after finishing the work in a wonderfully short space of time, called for more work. To get rid of his officious assistants, the farmer called outside the door that Dunruilg was on fire. The Fairies immediately rushed out in great haste and never came back.

In Mull, the Fairy residence is said to have been the bold headland in the southwest of the island known as Tòn Bhuirg. Some say the Elves were brought to the house by two old women, who were tired of spinning and incautiously said they wished all the people in Tòn Bhuirg were there to assist. According to others, the Elves were in the habit of coming to Tàpull House in the Ross of Mull, and their excessive zeal made them very unwelcome. In Skye the event is said to have occurred at Dùn Bhuirbh. There are two places of the name, one in Lyndale and one in Beinn-an-ùine, near Druimuighe, above Portree. The rhyme they had when they came to Tapull is known as "The Rhyme of the Goodman of Tapull's Servants" (*Rann gillean fir Thàbuill*).

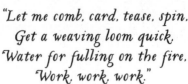

"*Let me comb, card, tease, spin,*
Get a weaving loom quick,
Water for fulling on the fire,
Work, work, work."

The cry they raised when going away, in the Skye version, is:

"*Dunsuirv on fire,*
Without dog or man,
My balls of thread
And my bags of meal."

A man on the farm of Kennovay in Tiree saw the Fairies, at about twelve o'clock at night, enter the house, glide round the room, and go out again. They said and did nothing.

The Lowland Fairies

"The people" had several dwellings near the village of Largs (*Na Leargun Gallta*, the slopes-near-the-sea of the strangers), on the coast of Ayrshire.

Knock Hill was full of Elves, and the site of the old Tron Tree, now the centre of the village, was a favourite haunt. A sow, belonging to the man who cut down the Tron Tree, was found dead in the byre next morning. A hawker, with a basket of crockery, was met near the Noddle Burn by a Fairy woman. She asked him for a bowl she pointed out in his basket, but he refused to give it to her. On coming to the top of a brae near the village, his basket tumbled, and all his dishes ran on edge to the foot of the incline. None were broken except the one he had refused to the Fairy. It was found in fragments. The same day, however, the hawker found a treasure that made up for his loss. That, said the person from whom the story was heard, was the custom of the Fairies: they never took anything without making up for it some other way.

On market days, they went about, stealing here and there a little of the wool or yarn set out for sale. A present of shoes and stockings made them give great assistance at outdoor work. A man was taken by them to a pump near the Haylee Toll, where he danced all night with them. A headless man was one of the company.

They often came to people's houses at night and were heard washing their children. If they found no water in the house, they washed them in *kit*, or sowen water. They were fond of spinning and weaving, and, if chided or thwarted, cut the weaver's webs at night. They one night dropped a child's cap, a very pretty article, in a weaver's house to which they had come to wash their children. They, however, took the cap away the following night.

93

In another instance, a band of four was heard crossing over the bedclothes. Two women went first, laughing, and two men followed, wondering if the women were far ahead of them.

A man cut a slip from an ash tree growing near a Fairy dwelling. On his way home in the evening, he stumbled and fell. He heard the Fairies give a laugh at his mishap. During the night he was hoisted away and could tell nothing of what had happened until, in the morning, he found himself in the byre, astride on a cow and holding on by its horns.

KINDNESS TO A NEGLECTED CHILD

The Elves sometimes took care of neglected children. The herder who tended the Baile-phuill cattle on Heynist Hill sat down one day on a green eminence (*cnoc*) in the hill, which had the reputation of being tenanted by the Fae. His son, a young child, was along with him. He fell asleep and, when he awoke, the child was not there. He roused himself and vowed aloud that unless his boy was restored, he would not leave a stone or clod of the hillock together. A voice from underground answered that the child was safe at home with his mother and that they (the "people") had taken him lest he should come to harm with the cold.

*Fairies comfort a sleeping child
who is lost and asleep in the forest.*

FAIRY GIFTS

A smith, the poorest workman in his trade, who only got coarse work to do because of his inferior skill, was known as the "Smith of Plough-shares." He was also the ugliest man and the rudest speaker. One day, he fell asleep on a hillock, and three Fairy women, coming that way, each left him a parting gift. After that, he became the best workman, the best-looking man, and the best speaker in the place, and he became known as the "Smith of Tales."

A man, out hunting, fell asleep in a dangerous place, near the brink of a precipice. When he awoke, a Fairy woman was sitting at his head, singing gently.

Fairies may impart magical powers and gifts to humans in their sleep.

FAIRY SUPERSTITIONS

Sleeping beside a Fairy hillock is the best
way to gain Fairy magic. Fairies are known
to bestow powers and gifts on people they
encounter, especially if they take pity
upon them or sense their struggle.

LIFTED, OR TAKEN, BY THE FAIRIES

Black Donald of the Multitude, as he was ever afterward known, was ploughing on the farm of Baile-pheutrais, on the island of Tiree, when a heavy shower came on from the west. In those days, it required at least two people to work a plough: one to hold it and one to lead the horses. Donald's companion took shelter to the lee of the team. When the shower passed, Donald himself was nowhere to be found, nor was he seen again till evening. He then came from an easterly direction, with his coat on his arm. He said the Fairies had taken him in an eddy wind to the islands to the north—Coll, Skye, etc. In proof of this, he said that a person (naming him) was dead in Coll, and people would be across the next day to Kennovay, a village on the other side of Baile-pheutrais where smuggling was carried on at the time, to get whisky for the funeral. This turned out to be the case. Donald said he had done no harm while away, except that the Fairies had made him throw an arrow at, and kill, a speckled cow in Skye. When crossing the sea, he was in great terror lest he should fall.

About twenty years ago, a cooper, employed on board a ship, landed at Martin's Isle near Coigeach, in Ross-shire, to cut brooms. He traversed the islet and then somehow fell asleep. He felt as if something were pushing him, and, on awakening, he found himself on the island of Rona, ten miles off. He cut the brooms, and with a shower of rain coming on, he again fell asleep. On waking, he found himself back on Martin's Isle. He could only, it is argued, have been transported back and forth by the Fairies.

A seer gifted with the second sight (*taibhseis*), a resident at Bousd, in the east end of Coll, was frequently lifted by Fairies that lived in a hillock in his neighbourhood. He told how, on one occasion, they took him to the sea-girt rock, called *Eileirig*, and after diverting themselves with him for an hour or two, took him home again. So he said himself.

A man who went to fish on Saturday afternoon at a rock in Kinnavara Hill (*Beinn Chinn-a-Bharra*), the extreme *west* point of Tiree, did not make his appearance at home until six o'clock the following morning. He said that after leaving the rock the evening before, he remembered nothing but passing a number of beaches. The white beaches of Tiree, from the surrounding land being a dead level, are at night the most noticeable features in the scenery. On coming to his senses, he found himself on the top of the dùn at Caolis in the extreme *east* end of the island, twelve miles from his starting point.

A few years ago, a man in Lismore, travelling at night with a web of cloth on his shoulder, lost his way, walked on all night without knowing where he was going, and in the morning was found among rocks, where he could never have made his way alone. He could give no account of himself, and his wanderings were universally ascribed to the Fairies.

Red Donald of the Fairies, as he was called (and the name stuck to him all his life), used to see the Fairies when he was a boy. He was the herder at the Spital above Dalnacardoch in Perthshire, and he was taken by them to his father's house at Ardlàraich in Rannoch, a distance of a dozen miles, through the night. In the morning, he was found sitting at the fireside, and, as the door was barred, he must have been let in by the chimney.

98

An old man in Achabeg, Morvern, went one night on a gossiping visit to a neighbour's house. It was wintertime, and a river near the place was flooded, which, in the case of a mountain torrent, means that it was impassable. The old man did not return home that night, and next morning was found near the shï-en of Luran na Leaghadh in Sasory, some distance across the river. He could give no account of how he got there, only that when on his way home, a storm came about him, and on coming to himself, he was where they had found him.

When Dr. M'Laurin was tenant of Invererragan, near Connal Ferry in Benderloch, "*Calum Clever*," who derived his name from his skills in singing tunes and in travelling (gifts given him by the Fairies), stayed with him whole nights. The doctor sent him to Fort William with a letter, telling him to procure the assistance of "his own people" and be back with an immediate answer. Calum asked as much time as one game at shinty would take and was back in the evening, before the game was finished. He never could have travelled the distance without Fairy aid.

FAIRY SUPERSTITIONS

It is believed that humans can be taken, or lifted, by Fairies to remote places where they could not have arrived on their own. They would wake in confusion, with no memory as to how they managed to arrive there.

TAKING AWAY COWS AND SHEEP

A farmer had two good cows that were seized one spring with some unaccountable malady. They ate any amount of food given them, but neither grew fat nor yielded milk. They lay on their sides and could not be made to rise. An old man in the neighbourhood advised that they should be hauled up the hill and rolled down its steepest and longest incline. The brutes, he said, were not the farmer's cows at all, but two old men the Fairies had substituted for them. The farmer acted on this advice and, at the bottom of the descent, down which the cows were sent rolling, nothing was found, neither cow nor man, either dead or alive.

An animal stolen by Fairies was believed to be tainted by their magic.

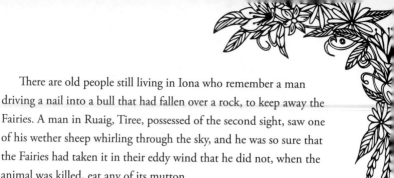

There are old people still living in Iona who remember a man driving a nail into a bull that had fallen over a rock, to keep away the Fairies. A man in Ruaig, Tiree, possessed of the second sight, saw one of his wether sheep whirling through the sky, and he was so sure that the Fairies had taken it in their eddy wind that he did not, when the animal was killed, eat any of its mutton.

DISTURBING OR DISCOVERING FAIRY DWELLINGS

An old man kept a green hillock near his house, on which he frequently reclined in summer, very clean, sweeping away any filth or cow or horse droppings he might find on it. One evening, as he sat on the hillock, a little man, a stranger to him, came and thanked him for his care of the hillock and added that if at any time the village cattle should leave their enclosure during the night, he and his friends would show their gratitude by keeping them from the old man's crops. The Fairy promise, being tested, was found good.

Hills such as Schiehallion in Perthshire, and Ben-y-ghloe in Argyllshire, the "Fairy dwelling of tempestuous weather" in Morvern and Dunniquoich (the bowl-shaped hill), and Dùn-deacainn and Shien-sloy (the multitude's residence), near Inverary, have the reputation of being tenanted by Fairies. The three latter hills are in sight of each other.

A native of the Island of Coll went to pull some wild briar plants. He tried to pull one growing in the face of a rock. When he made the first tug, he heard someone calling to him from the inside of the rock, and he ran away without ever looking back. To this day, he says no one need try to persuade him there are no Fairies, for he heard them himself.

Be cautious when weeding of disturbing Fairy homes. Wild briar plants, in particular, should not be pulled from rocky surfaces as they are often used to conceal the entrance to a Fairy home.

A shepherd at Lochaweside, coming home with a wether sheep on his back, saw an open cave in the face of a rock where he had never noticed a cave before. He laid down his burden and, stepping over to the entrance of the cave, stuck his knife into a fissure of the rock that formed a side of the entrance. He then leisurely looked in and saw the cave full of guns and arms and chests studded with brass nails, but no appearance of tenants. Happening to turn his head for a moment to look at the sheep, and seeing it about to move off, he allowed the knife to move from its place. On looking again at the rock, he only saw water trickling from the fissure from which the knife had been withdrawn.

A person who had a green knoll in front of his house and was in the habit of throwing out dirty water at the door was told by the Fairies to move the door to the other side of the house, as the water was spoiling their furniture and utensils. He did this, and he and the Fairies lived on good terms ever after.

In the evening (and this is a story worth telling twice), a man was tethering his horse on a grassy mound. A head appeared out of the ground, and told him to drive his tether pin somewhere else, as he

A Fairy carving new tools from her nook in a stone wall.

was letting the rain into their house, and had nearly killed one of the inmates by driving the peg into his ear.

Beinn Feall is one of the most prominent hills on the Island of Coll. It is highly esteemed for the excellence of its pasture, and it was of old much frequented by the Fairies. A fisherman going to his occupation at night saw it covered with green silk, spread out to dry, and heard all night the sound of a quern (handmill) at work inside. On another occasion, similar sounds were heard in the same hill, and voices singing:

> *"Though good the haven we left,*
> *Seven times better the haven we found."*

A man who avoided tethering horse or cow on a Fairy hillock near his house, or in any way breaking the green sward that covered it, was rewarded by the Fairies' driving his horse and cow to the lee of the hillock on stormy nights.

103

FAIRY ASSISTANCE AND BEHAVIOR

While many Fairies are eager to offer gifts, there are plenty of stories relating encounters where Fairies displayed erratic or dangerous behavior.

A man in Flodigarry, an islet near Skye, expressed a wish for his corn to be reaped, though it should be by Fairy assistance. The Fairies came and reaped the field in two nights. They were seen at work, seven score and fifteen of them. After reaping the field, they called for more work, and the man set them to empty the sea.

One of the chiefs of Dowart was hurried with his harvest, likely to lose his crop for want of shearers. He sent word through all of Mull for assistance. A little old man came and offered himself. He asked as wages only the full of a straw-rope he had with him of corn when the work was over. M'Lean formed no high opinion of the little man, but as the work was urgent and the remuneration trifling, he engaged his services. He placed him along with another old man and an old woman on a ridge by themselves, and he told them never to worry if they fell behind the rest; they should take it easy and not fatigue themselves. The little man, however, soon made his assistants leave the way, and he set them to making sheaf-bands. He finished shearing that ridge before the rest of the shearers were halfway done with theirs, and no fault could be found with the manner in which the work was done. M'Lean would not part with the little reaper till the end of harvest. Fuller payment was offered for his excellent services, but he refused to take more than had been bargained for. He began putting the corn in the rope, and put in all that was in the field, then all that was in the stackyard, and finally all that was in the barn. He said this would do just now, tightened the rope, and lifted the burden on his back. He

Fairies are believed to love planting and harvesting fruit and other crops.

was setting off with it, when M'Lean, in despair, cried out, "Tuesday I ploughed, Tuesday I sowed, Tuesday I reaped; thou who did'st ordain the three Tuesdays, suffer not all that is in the rope to leave me." "The hand of your father and grandfather be upon you!" said the little man. "It is well that you spoke."

Another version of the tale was told in Morvern. A servant, engaged in spring by a man who lived at Aodienn Mòr ("Big Face") in Liddesdale, when told to begin ploughing, merely thrust a walking-stick into the ground and, holding it to his nose, said the earth was not yet ready (*cha robh an talamh air dàir fathast*). This went on until the neighbours were more than half-finished with their spring work. His master then peremptorily ordered the work to be done. By the next morning, all of Big Face was ploughed, sown, and harrowed. The shearing of the crop was done in the same mysterious and expeditious manner. The servant had the association-craft, which secured the assistance of the Fairies. When getting his wages, the Fairy was like to take away the whole crop, and the farmer got rid of him as in the previous version.

FAIRY-TRACKING TIP

Keeping a garden in your yard increases your chance of spotting a Fairy at work. Consider leaving a bag of seeds out by your garden and waiting to see if a magical creature might be tempted to sow them for you.

An old man in Còrnaig, Tiree, went to sow his croft, or piece of land. He was scarce of seed oats, but putting the little he had in a circular dish made of plaited straw, called *plàdar*, suspended from his shoulder by a strap (*iris*), commenced operations. His son followed, harrowing the seed. The old man went on sowing long after the son expected the seed corn was exhausted. He made some remark expressive of his wonder, and the old man said, "Evil befall you, why did you speak? I might have finished the field if you had held your tongue, but now I cannot go further," and he stopped. The piece sown would properly take four times as much seed as had been used.

A man in the Ross of Mull, about to sow his land, filled a sheet with seed oats and commenced. He went on sowing, but the sheet remained full. At last, a neighbour took notice of the strange phenomenon and said, "The face of your evil and iniquity be upon you; is the sheet never to be empty?" When this was said, a little brown bird leapt out of the sheet, and the supply of corn ceased. The bird was called *Torc Sona* ("Happy Hog"), and when any of the man's descendants fall in with any luck, they are asked if the *Torc Sona* still follows the family.

A man in the Braes of Portree, in Skye, with a large but weak family, had his spring and harvest work done by the Fairies. No one could tell how it was done, but somehow it was finished as soon as that of any of his neighbours. All his family, however, grew up "peculiar in their minds."

FAIRY SUPERSTITIONS

If you see a brown bird while tilling the land, planting grass, or gardening, it might be a sign that a Fairy has blessed you and bestowed on you good luck and the promise of an abundant harvest.

A kind Fairy feeding a bird its dinner.

Bean Shith, *Elle Woman, or Woman of Peace*

While supper was being prepared in a farmer's house in Morvern, a very little woman, a stranger to the residents, entered. She was invited to share supper with the family but would take none of the food of which the meal consisted or of any other they had to offer. She said her people lived on the tops of heather, in the loch called *Lochan Fasta Litheag*. There does not seem to be any loch of that name in Morvern.

A Fairy at home on the top of a heather plant.

The name is difficult to translate but indicates a lakelet covered with weeds or green scum. The little woman left the house as she came, and fear kept everyone from following her or questioning her further.

A woman at Kinloch Teagus, in the same parish, was sitting on a summer day in front of the house, preparing green dye by boiling heather tops and alum together. This preparation is called *ailmeid*. A young woman, whom she had never seen before, came to her and asked for something to eat. The stranger was dressed in green and wore a cap bearing the appearance of the king's hood of a sheep. The housewife said the family were at the pasture with the cattle, and there was no food in the house; there was not even a drink of milk. The visitor then asked to be allowed to make brose of the dye, and she received permission to do what she liked with it. She was asked where she stayed, and she said, "In this same neighbourhood." She drank off the compost and rushed away, throwing three somersaults, and disappeared.

A young man named Callum, when crossing the rugged hills of Ard-meadhonach ("Middle Height") in Mull, fell in with some St. John's wort (*Achlusan Challum-chille*), a plant of magic powers if found when neither sought nor wanted. He took some of it with him. He had *dùcun* (small swellings below the toes) on his feet, and on coming to a stream sat down and bathed them in the water. Looking up, he saw an ugly little woman, having no nostrils, on the other side of the stream, with her feet resting against his own. She asked him for the plant he had in his hand, but he refused to give it. She asked him to make snuff of it and then give her some. He thought, *What could she want with snuff, when she had no nostril to put it in?* He left her and went further on. As he did not come home that night, his friends and neighbours went in search of him through the hills the next day. He was found by his father, asleep on the side of a *cnoc*, a small hillock, and when awakened, he thought, from the position of the sun, he had only slept a few minutes. He had, in fact, slept for twenty-four hours. His dog lay sleeping in the hollow between his two shoulders and had "neither hair nor fur" on. It is supposed it had lost its hair in chasing away the Fairies and protecting its master.

FAIRY SUPERSTITIONS

According to Fairy lore, one way to identify a Fairy is to check for nostrils. The absence of any, or the presence of just one, is an indicator of Fairy lineage.

A herdsman at Baile-phuill, in the west end of Tiree, fell asleep on Cnoc Ghrianal, at the eastern base of Heynish Hill, on a fine summer afternoon. He was awakened by a violent slap on the ear. On rubbing his eyes and looking up, he saw a woman, the most beautiful he had ever seen, in a green dress, with a brooch fastening it at the neck, walking away from him. She went westward, and he followed her for some distance, but she vanished—he could not tell how.

Iona Banshi

A man in Iona, thinking daylight had come, rose and went to a rock to fish. After catching some fish, he observed he had been misled by the clearness of the moonlight, and he set off home. On the way, as the night was so fine, he sat down to rest himself on a hillock. He fell asleep and was awakened by the pulling of the fishing rod, which he had in his hand. He found the rod was being pulled in one direction and the fish in another. He secured both, and was making off, when he heard sounds behind him as of a woman weeping. On his turning around to her, she said, "Ask news, and you will get news." He answered, "I put God between us." When he said this, she caught him and thrashed him soundly. Every night after, he was compelled to meet her, and on her repeating the same words and his giving the same answer, was similarly drubbed. To escape from her persecutions, he went to the Lowlands. When engaged there cutting drains, he saw a raven on the bank above him. This proved to be his tormentor, and he was compelled to meet her again at night, and, as usual, she thrashed him. He resolved to go to America. On the eve of his departure, his Fairy mistress met him and said, "You are going away to escape from me. If you see a hooded crow when you land, I am that crow." On landing in America, he saw a crow sitting in a tree and knew it to be his old enemy.

111

A Fairy summoning mist.

The Wife of Ben-y-Ghloe

Donald and Big John (*Dòmhnull's Iain mòr*) were out deer hunting on the lofty mountain of Ben-y-ghloe, in Athol in Perthshire, when a heavy snowstorm came on, and they lost their way. They came to a hut in a hollow and entered. The only one there was an old woman, the like of whom they said they had never seen. Her two arms were bare, of great length, and grizzled and sallow to look at. She neither asked them to come in nor go out, and being much in need of shelter, they went in and sat at the fire. There was a look in her eye that might "terrify a coward," and she hummed a surly song, the words of which were unintelligible to them. They asked for meat, and she set before them a fresh salmon trout, saying, "Little you thought I would give you your dinner today." She also said she could do more, and that it was she who had clothed the hill with mist to make them come to her house. They stayed with her all night. She was very kind and hospitable. She told her name to them when they were leaving, that she was the "wife of Ben-y-Ghloe." They could not say whether she was *sìth* or *saoghalta* (Fae or human), but they never visited her again.

If you're on a Fairy walk, and you see a hooded crow, it could actually be a spying Fairy in disguise, surveying whether or not you are dangerous before approaching.

FAIRIES AND ANIMALS

It has been said that Fairies have the ability to communicate with animals, to shapeshift into the forms of animals, and to drink their milk.

Fairies and Goats

In Breadalbane and the Highlands of Perthshire, it is said the Fairies live on goats' milk. A goat was taken home by a man in Strathfillan, in Perthshire, to be killed. In the evening, a stranger, dressed in green, came to the door. The man asked the stranger to come in and rest himself. The stranger said he could not, as he was in a hurry and on his way to Dunbuck (a celebrated Fairy haunt near Dunbarton), an urgent message having come for him. He said that many a day that goat had kept him in milk. He then disappeared. He could be nothing but a Fairy.

Fairies and Cows

A strong-minded, headstrong woman in Kianish, Tiree, had a cow, the milk of which strangely failed. Suspecting that the cow was being milked by someone during the night, she sat up and watched. She saw

a woman dressed in green coming noiselessly and milking the cow. She came behind and caught her. In explanation, the Fairy woman said she had a child sick with smallpox, and, as a favour, she asked to be allowed to milk the cow for one month, until the child got better. This was allowed, and when the month was out, the cow's milk became as plentiful as ever.

A Fairy woman milking a cow.

That the Fairies took away cows at night to milk them and then sent them back in the morning was a belief in Craignish, Morvern, Tiree, Lochaber, and probably in the whole Highlands. When milk lost its virtue, and yielded neither cream, nor butter, nor cheese, the work was that of witches and other such diabolical agencies. When the mischief was done by the Fairies, the whole milk disappeared.

There was a Fairy hillock near Dowart, in Mull, close to the road that led from the cattle fold to the village. If any milk was spilt by the dairy-maids on their way home with the milk pails, it was a common saying that the Fairies would get its benefit.

Fairy Cows

A strong man named Dugald Campbell was one night watching the cattle on the farm of Baile-phuill, in the west of Tiree. A little red cow came among the herd and was attacked by the other cows. It fled, and they followed. Dugald also set off in pursuit. Sometimes the little red cow seemed near; sometimes far away. At last, it entered the face of a rock, and one of the other cows followed and was never again seen. The whole herd would have followed had Dugald not intercepted them.

A poor person's cow, in Skye, was by some act of oppression taken from him. That night, the Fairies brought him another cow, remarkable only in having green water weeds upon it. This cow thrived.

Some generations ago, cows came ashore on Nisibost beach, on the farm of Loscantire (*Losg-an-tir*), in Harris. The people got between them and the shore, with whatever weapons they could get, and kept them from returning to the sea again. Even handfuls of sand thrown between the cows and the shore kept them back. These sea-cows were in all respects like ordinary Highland cattle, but they were supposed to live under the sea on the seaweed called *meillich*. They were called

Fairy cows (*Cro sìth*), and the superiority of the Loscantire cattle was said to have originated from them. It is more probable that the superiority of the stock was the origin of the Fairy cattle.

Fairies and Dogs

A woman, near Portree, in Skye, was coming home in the evening with her milk pails from the cattle fold, accompanied by a dog, which went trotting along before her. Suddenly, the dog was observed to run to a green hillock, fall down on its knees, and hold its ear to the ground. The woman went up to see what the matter was and, on listening, heard a woman inside the hillock churning milk and singing at her work. At the end of every verse, there was a chorus or exclamation of *hŭ*. The song was learnt by the listener and became known as the "Song of the Hillock."

FAIRY-TRACKING TIP

Although Fairies seem to be startled by and afraid of dogs, this does not always mean that you should leave your dog at home when you go on a Fairy-tracking mission. There are dogs who are uniquely skilled at sniffing out Fairy dwellings, finding hillocks, and hearing the sounds of Fairy activity underground.

A young Fairy tracker being spied on by hidden Fairies.

FAIRY MUSIC

Two children, a brother and sister, went on a moonlight winter's night to Kennavarra Hill to look after a snare they had set for little birds in a hollow near a stream. The ground was covered with snow, and when the two descended into the hollow, they heard the most beautiful music coming from underground, close to where they were standing. In the extremity of terror, both fled. The boy went fastest and never looked behind him. The girl was at first encumbered by her father's big shoes, which she had put on for the occasion, but, throwing them off, she reached home with a panting heart, not long after her brother. She told this story when she was an old woman. She had never forgotten the fright the Fairy music gave her in childhood.

In the Braes of Portree, there is a hillock called "The Fairy Dwelling of the Pretty Hill." A man passing near it in the evening heard from underground the most delightful music ever heard. He could not, however, tell the exact spot from which the sound emanated.

Sounds of exquisite music, as if played by a piper marching at the head of a procession, used to be heard going underground from the Harp Hillock to the top of the dùn of Caolis, in the east end of Tiree. Many tunes, whatever be their musical merit, said to have been learned from the Fairies, can be heard. One of these, which the writer heard, seemed to consist entirely of variations upon the word "do-leedl'em."

CHAPTER 3

Other Magical Beings

"The Neck here his harp in the glass-castle plays,
And Mermaidens comb out
their green hair always,
And bleach here their shining white clothes."

LONG-AGO TALES FROM SCOTLAND, ENGLAND,
IRELAND, SCANDINAVIA, AND BEYOND ADD
FODDER TO OUR IMAGINATION WITH THEIR
ADDITION OF UNIQUELY MAGICAL BEASTS
THAT GUARD, HARVEST, AND INHABIT THE
LAND ALONG WITH US. THESE ANCIENT
FIGURES REMIND US TO STAY CURIOUS ABOUT
THE NATURAL WORLD AND TO BELIEVE
BEYOND WHAT OUR EYES CAN DISCERN. THE
REWARD OF OUR CURIOSITY AND RESEARCH
IS TO UNCOVER MYSTERIES AND MYSTICAL
CREATURES BEYOND OUR IMAGINING.

THE GLAISTIG

The Glaistig was a tutelary (guardian) in the shape of a thin, grey little woman, with long yellow hair reaching to her heels, dressed in green, haunting certain sites or farms, and watching over the house or the cattle. She is called the "Green Glaistig" from her wan looks and dress of green, the characteristic Fairy colour. She is said to have been at first a woman of honourable position, a former mistress of the house, who had been put under enchantments and now had a Fairy nature given her. She disliked dogs and took fools and people of weak intellect under her particular charge. She was solitary in her habits, not more than one, unless when accompanied by her own young one, being found in the same haunt. Her strength was very great, much greater than that of any Fairy, and one yell of hers was sufficient to waken the echoes of distant hills. Some would deny being afraid of her, but ordinarily people were afraid of meeting her. She might do them a mischief and leave them a token, by which they would have cause to remember the encounter. She made herself generally useful, but, in many cases, she was only mischievous and troublesome.

She seems in all cases to have had a special interest in the cows and the dairy, and to have resented any want of recognition of her services. A portion of milk was set apart for her every evening, in a hole for the purpose in some convenient stone; and unless this was done, something was found amiss in the dairy the next morning. Others left milk for her only when leaving the summer pastures for the season.

She was seldom seen, although when anything was to happen to the house, she followed. She might then be seen making her way in the evening up the slope to the castle, herding the cattle on the pastures, sunning herself on the top of a distant rock, or coming to

A Glaistig (Banshi) standing guard over a castle.

the fold at dusk for her allowance of milk. Her cries and the noises she made while arranging the furniture, shouting after the cattle, or at the approach of joy or sorrow, were frequently heard.

In the south Highlands, the Glaistig was represented as a little wan woman, stout and not tall, but very strong. In Skye, where most of her duties were assigned to a deity, the Gruagach, she was said to be very tall, "a lath of a body," like a white reflection or shade.

Her name is derived from *glas*, which means grey, wan, or pale-green, and *stìg*, which is a sneaking or crouching object, probably in allusion to her invisibility, noiseless motions, or small size. In the *Highland Society's Dictionary*, she is called "a she-devil, or hag, in the shape of a goat," and the definition was accepted by M'Leod and Dewar. This, however, is a mistake. The shape of a goat, in the Highlands as elsewhere, has been assigned to the devil only, and there was nothing diabolical, or of the nature of an evil spirit, seeking the perdition of mankind, ascribed to the poor Glaistig. She occupied a middle position between the Fairies and mankind; she was not a Fairy woman, but one of human race who had a Fairy nature given to her. The Fairies themselves are much nearer in character to the race of man than to that of devils. Of course, all unearthly beings are to be treated with caution, but of all the beings with which fear or fancy has peopled the unseen world, the Glaistig and her near relation, the Brownie, are among the most harmless.

The house- or castle-haunting Glaistig was also known by the names *Maighdean sheòmbair* ("chamber-maid") or *Gruagach* (young woman or long-haired

A Highlands castle fit for a Glaistig.

one), and her attachment was not to the family but to the site or stance (*làrach*). It was always the abodes of the affluent in which she resided, and she continued her occupancy after a change of tenants, and even after the building was deserted and had become a nesting place for wild birds. In olden times, there was a perpetuity of tenure enjoyed by large tenants, and it is not surprising that writers have fallen into the mistake of supposing the tutelary guardian of the house to be that of its tenants.

The Glaistig had sympathy with the tenant so far that she broke out into loud expressions of joy or sorrow, or made appearances more frequently when happiness or misfortune were to come upon the family, but her real attachment was to the building or site. Indeed, none of these beings of superstition were tutelary to the human race or had anything about them of the character of the genius or evil spirit. When the house was to be levelled, even though the family remained on the land and a new house (on another site) was built, the Glaistig made a lamentable outcry, left, and was never afterward seen or heard. Her usual occupation consisted in "putting things in order" at night, sweeping the floor, moving chairs and tables about, and arranging the furniture. After the household had retired to rest, she was heard at work in locked apartments in which no human being could be. It was then known there would shortly be an arrival of strangers.

In the morning, in most cases, the furniture was found untouched or out of place. In other cases, the house was found tidied up, and work that had been left for the Glaistig, such as washing, was found finished. She was fond of working with the spinning wheel, and, according to some, it was to prevent her coming to the house, and working with it on Sundays that old women were careful to take off the band every Saturday night. She had a similar fondness for working with tradesmen's tools, and artisans were often very annoyed at hearing her working at night, then finding their tools spoiled or mislaid in the morning. When the servants neglected their work or spoke disrespectfully of her, or did anything to her favourites, she played pranks to punish them. She knocked down the water basins, misarranged the bedclothes, put dust in the meat, led the objects of her resentment in a fool's chase about the house, or in the dark gave them a slap to be remembered on the side of the head. When happiness or misfortune, a marriage or a death, was to occur in the household, she was heard rejoicing or wailing long before the event occurred.

It was, however, to the being of this class that haunted the folds of the cattle that the name *Glaistig* is most commonly given. Her occupation consisted in a general oversight of the sheep, cows, and horses of the farm. When the family was at dinner, or the herdsman had fallen asleep and neglected his charge, she kept the cattle out of mischief; though not seen, she was heard shouting after them and driving them to their proper pastures. In this respect, she behaved like an old and careful herdsman. If the cows were not milked clean, she punished the dairy-maid by some unchancy prank. At night, she kept the calves from the cows (a useful and necessary occupation before the days of enclosures and plentiful farm accommodation) and its substance in the milk. In summer, she accompanied the cattle to the hill pastures and there had her portion of milk duly poured out for her in the evening in a stone near the fold. Unless this was done, the calves would be found the next morning with the cows, the cream would not rise from the milk, a cow would be found dead, or some other mishap would occur.

She was not supposed ever to enter a house but to stay in a ravine (*eas*) near a Fairy residence. She disliked dogs very much, and if a present of shoes or clothes was made to her, she was offended and left. She is not generally spoken of as appearing in any shape but her own,

125

A Glaistig may appear in the form of an old grey mare.

but in some localities and tales, she is said to assume the shape of a horse (an "old grey mare") or even of a dog.

The Glaistig resembled the Fae in being invisible and in having a noiseless gliding motion; in her dislike of dogs; in affecting green in her dress; in being addicted to meddling at night with the spinning wheel and tradesmen's tools; in her outcries being a premonition of coming events; in being kept away by steel; and in her ability to give skills in handicrafts to her favourites. The Fairies bestowed this skill on those who had the *Ceaird-Chomuinn*, or association-craft, *i.e.*, the assistance of "the folk." The Glaistig gave the choice of "ingenuity without advantage" (*ealdhain gun rath*) or "advantage without ingenuity" (*rath gun ealdhain*). Those who chose the former proved clever workmen but never prospered; those who chose the latter turned out to be stupid fellows who made fortunes.

She differed in being more akin to human women than the true Fairy wife (*Bean shìth*); she was stronger and, as it were, more substantial. Though her "bed" was near a Fairy dwelling, and she could command the services of the Elves, she did not engage in Fairy employments or recreations. The Fairies punished people of a discontented, grumbling disposition by taking away the substance of their goods. The Glaistig was also offended at littleness and meanness of mind, but meanness of a different kind. Those who looked down on fools and people of weak intellect, or ill treated them, she paid off by putting dust or soot in their meat. Akin to this was her punishment of neglect toward servants.

THE BROWNIE

The term *Brùnaidh*, signifying a supernatural being haunting the abodes of the affluent and doing work for the servants, seems to have made its way into the Highlands more recently and along with south country ideas. This name is generally applied only to a big, corpulent, clumsy man, and in many districts it has no other meaning. Its derivation is Teutonic, not Celtic, and Brownies are mostly heard of in places where southern ideas have penetrated (such as the south of Argyllshire) or where, as in the Orkneys and Shetland, a Teutonic race is settled.

In the islet of Càra, on the west of Cantyre, the old house, once belonging to the Macdonalds, was haunted by a Brownie that drank milk, made a terrific outcry when hurt, and disliked the Campbell race. In the old castle of Largie, on the opposite coast of Cantyre, which belonged to the same Macdonalds, there was also a Brownie that was supposed to be the same as the Càra one. Since the modern house was built, the Brownie has not been seen or heard. In Càra, he is still occasionally heard. It is not known exactly what he is like, as no one has ever seen more than a glimpse of him.

Before the arrival of strangers, he would put the house in order. He disliked anything dirty being left in the house for the night. Dirty bedclothes were put out by him before morning.

He was much addicted to giving slaps in the dark to those who soiled the house; and there are some who can testify to receiving slaps that left their faces bruised. He tumbled on the water basins left full overnight. A man was lifted out of bed by him and found himself "bare naked," on awakening at the fireside. A woman, going late in the evening for her cows, found that the Brownie had been there before her and had tied them securely in the barn.

In one of the castles in the centre of Argyllshire, a Brownie came to the bedside of a servant woman who had retired for the night, arranged the blankets, and, pulling them above her, said, "Take your sleep, poor creature." He then went away.

In character, the Brownie was harmless, but he made mischief unless every place was left open at night. He was fed with warm milk by the dairy-maid.

A native of the Shetland Isles writes me that the Brownie was well known in that locality. He worked about the barn, and at night ground grain with the handmill for those to whom he was attached. He could grind a bag or two of grain in a night. He was once rewarded for his labours by a cloak and hood left for him at the mill. The articles were gone in the morning, and the Brownie never came back, hence the following saying:

"When he got his cloak and hood,
He did no more good."

The same story is told of Brownies in the Scottish Lowlands, and of one in Strathspey, who said, when he went away:

"Brownie has got a coat and cap,
Brownie will do no more work."

A Brownie delights in putting the house in order.

The Brownie, according to Thomas Keightley in his 1892 book, *The Fairy Mythology*, is a personage of small stature and wrinkled visage; covered with short, curly brown hair; and wearing a brown mantle and hood. Another name by which the domestic spirit was known in some parts of Scotland was Shellycoat, of which the origin is uncertain. His residence is the hollow of an old tree, a ruined castle, or the abode of humans. He is attached to particular families with whom he has been known to reside, even for centuries, threshing the corn, cleaning the house, and doing everything done by his northern and English brethren. He is, to a certain degree, disinterested; like many great personages, he is shocked at anything approaching a bribe or douceur, yet, like them, he allows his scruples to be overcome if the thing be done in a genteel, delicate, and secret way. Thus, offer the Brownie a piece of bread, a cup of drink, or a new coat and hood, and he would perhaps disappear in a huff, leaving the place forever, but leave a nice bowl of cream and some fresh honeycomb in a snug, private corner, and the provisions would soon disappear, though the Brownie, it was to be supposed, never knew anything of them.

A good woman had just made a web of linsey-woolsey and, prompted by her good nature, had manufactured from it a snug mantle and hood for her little Brownie. Not content with laying the

129

gift in one of his favourite spots, she indiscreetly called to tell him it was there. This was too direct, and Brownie quitted the place, crying, "A new mantle and a new hood! Poor Brownie! Ye'll ne'er do mair gude!"

The Brownie was not without some roguery in his composition. Two lasses, having made a fine bowlful of buttered brose, had taken it into the byre to sup in the dark. In their haste, they had brought but one spoon, so, placing the bowl between them, they supped by turns.

"I hae got but three sups," cried the one, "and it's a' dune."

"It's a' dune, indeed," cried the other.

"Ha, ha, ha!" cried a third voice, "Brownie has got the maist o' it."

And the Brownie it was who had placed himself between them and gotten two sups for their one.

THE NIS

The Nis is the same being that is called the Kobold in Germany, the Brownie in Scotland, and whom we shall meet in various other places under different appellations. He is in Denmark and Norway also called Nisse god-dreng ("Nissè good lad"), and in Sweden Tomtgubbe ("Old Man of the House") or, briefly, Tomte.

He is evidently of the Dwarf family, as he resembles them in appearance and, like them, has the command of money and the same dislike of noise and tumult. He is the size of a year-old child but has the face of an old man. His usual dress is grey, with a pointed red cap, but on Michaelmas Day, he wears a round hat like those of the peasants.

No farmhouse goes on well unless there is a Nis in it, and well is it for the men and the women when they are in his good favour. They may go to their beds and give themselves no trouble about their work, and yet, in the morning, they will find the kitchen swept up, water brought in, and the horses cleaned and curried in the stable—and perhaps a supply of corn cribbed for them from the neighbours' barns. But he punishes them for any irregularity that takes place.

The Nisses of Norway, we are told, are fond of the moonlight, and in the wintertime they may be seen jumping over the yard or driving in sledges. They are also skilled in music and dancing and will, it is said, give instructions on the fiddle for a grey sheep, like the Swedish Strömkarl.

Every church, too, has its Nis, who looks to order and chastises those who misbehave themselves. He is called the Kirkegrim.

THE GUNNA

In olden times, the tillage in Tiree was in common, the crop was raised here and there throughout the farm, and the herding was in consequence very difficult to do. In Baugh, or on some farm in the west of the island (tradition is not uniform as to the locality), the cows were left in the pastures at night and were kept from the crops by some invisible herdsman. No one ever saw this hob-like being of the Highlands called a Gunna, and no one knew whence he came nor when he went away or whither he went. A *taibhseir*, or seer (one who had the second sight or sight of seeing ghosts), remained awake to see how the cattle were kept. He saw a man without clothes after them and, taking pity upon the man, made him a pair of trews (trousers) and a pair of shoes. When the ghostly herdsman put the trews on, he said (and his name became known for the first time):

"Trews upon Gunna,
Because Gunna does the herding,
But may Gunna never enjoy his trews,
If he tends cattle any more."

When he said this, he went away and was never again heard of. As previously mentioned, beings of this class seem to have had a great objection to presents of clothes.

A pair of shoes made the Glaistig at Unimore leave; a cap, coat, and breeches the Phynnodderee in the Isle of Man; in the Black Forest of Germany, a new coat drove away a Nix, one of the little water-people, with green teeth, that came and worked with the people all day; and Brownies, as already mentioned, in several places.

THE URISK

The Urisk was a large lubberly supernatural, of solitary habits and harmless character, that haunted lonely and mountainous places. Some identify him with the Brownie, but he differs from the fraternity of tutelary beings in having his dwelling not in the houses or haunts of humans but in solitudes and remote localities. There were male and female Urisks, and the race was said to be the offspring of unions between mortals and Fairies, that is, of the *leannan sìth*.

The Urisk was usually seen in the evening, big and grey (*mòr glas*), sitting on top of a rock and peering at the intruders on its solitude. The wayfarer whose path led along the mountainside, whose shattered rocks are loosely sprinkled, or along some desert moor, and who hurried for the fast-approaching nightfall, saw the Urisk sitting motionless on top of a rock, gazing at him or her or slowly moving out of the way. It spoke to some people and is even said to have thrashed them, but usually it did not meddle with the passersby. On the contrary, it at times gave a safe convoy to those who were belated.

In the Highlands of Breadalbane, the Urisk was said, in summertime, to stay in remote

A Urisk sitting upon a rock.

corries and on the highest parts of certain hills. In wintertime, it came down to the strath and entered certain houses at night to warm itself and then do some work for the farmer, such as grinding, thrashing, etc. Its presence was a sign of prosperity; it was said to leave comfort behind. Like the Brownie, it liked milk and good food, and a present of clothes drove it away.

An Urisk, haunting *Beinn Doohrain* (a hill beloved of the Celtic muse) on the confines of Argyllshire and Perthshire, stayed in summertime near the top of the hill, and in winter came down to the straths. A waterfall near the village of Clifton at Tyndrum, where it stayed on these occasions, is still called *Eas na h-ùruisg*, the Urisk's cascade. It was encountered by St. Fillan, who had his abode in a neighbouring strath and banished the Urisk to Rome.

The Urisk of Ben Loy (*Beinn Laoigh*, the "Calf's Hill"), also on the confines of these counties, came down in winter from his lofty haunts to the farm of Sococh, in Glen Orchy, which lies at the base of the mountain. It entered the house at night by the chimney, and it is said that on one occasion, the bar from which the chimney chain was suspended and on which the Urisk laid its weight in descending, had been taken away, causing the poor supernatural to have a bad fall.

It was fond of staying in a cleft at Moraig waterfall, and its labours in keeping the waters from falling too fast over the rock might be seen by anyone. A stone, on which it sat with its feet dangling over the fall, is called "Urisk stone" (*Clach na h-ùruisg*). The Urisk sometimes watched the herds of Sococh farm.

A man passing through Strath Duuisg, near Loch Sloy, at the head of Loch Lomond, on a keen frosty night, heard a Urisk on one side of the glen calling out, "Frost, frost, frost" ("*reoth, reoth, reoth*"). This was answered by another Urisk calling from the other side of

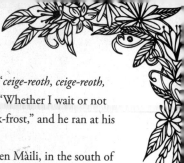

the glen, "Kick-frost, kick-frost, kick-frost" ("*ceige-reoth, ceige-reoth, ceige-reoth*"). The man, on hearing this, said, "Whether I wait or not for frost, I will never while I live wait for kick-frost," and he ran at his utmost speed until he was out of the glen.

The Urisk of the "Yellow Waterfall" in Glen Màili, in the south of Inverness-shire, used to come late every evening to a woman by the name of Mary and would sit and watch her plying her distaff without saying a word. A man, hoping to get a glimpse of the Urisk, put on Mary's clothes and sat in her place, twirling the distaff as best he could. The Urisk came to the door but would not enter. It said:

"I see your eye, I see your nose,
I see your great broad beard,
And though you will work the distaff,
I know you are a man."

The Urisk, like the Brownie of England, had great simplicity of character, and many tricks were played upon it in consequence. A farmer in Strathglass got it to undergo a painful operation that it might become fat and sleek like the farmer's own geldings. The weather at the time being frosty, it made a considerable outcry for some time after.

From its haunting lonely places, other appearances must often have been confounded with it. In Strathfillan, in the Highlands of Perthshire, a number of boys saw what was popularly said to be an Urisk. On the hill, when the sun was setting, something like a human being was seen sitting on the top of a large boulder, growing bigger and bigger until they fled. There is no difficulty in connecting this appearance with the circumstance that some sheep disappeared that year unaccountably from the hill, as well as a quantity of grain from the barn of the farm.

In the Hebrides, there is very little mention of the Urisk at all. In Tiree, the only trace of it is in the name of a hollow, Slochd an Aoirisg, through which the public road passes near the south shore. The belief that the Urisk assisted the farmer was not common anywhere, and all over the Highlands, the word ordinarily conveys no other idea than that which has been well defined as "a being supposed to haunt lonely and sequestered places, as mountain rivers and waterfalls."

THE BLUE MEN

The fallen angels were driven out of Paradise in three divisions: one became the Fairies on the land; one the Blue Men in the sea; and one the Nimble Men (*Fir Chlis*), *i.e.,* the Northern Streamers (Northern Lights) or Merry Dancers, in the sky. This explanation belongs to the North Hebrides and was heard by the writer in Skye. In Argyllshire, the Blue Men are unknown, and there is no mention of the Merry Dancers being congeners of the Fairies. The person who revealed this information was very positive he had himself seen one of the Blue Men. A blue-coloured man with a long grey face, floating from the waist out of the water, followed the boat in which he was for a long time and was occasionally so near that the observer might have put his hand upon him.

A Blue Man asleep on the waters.

The channel between Lewis and the Shant Isles (*Na h-Eileinean siant*, the "Charmed Islands") is called the "Stream of the Blue Men" (*Sruth nam Fear Gorm*). A ship, passing through it, came upon a blue-coloured man sleeping on the waters. He was taken on board, and, being thought of mortal race, strong twine was coiled around and around him from his feet to his shoulders until it seemed impossible for him to struggle or to move foot or arm. The ship had not gone far when two men were observed coming after it on the waters. One of them was heard to say, "Duncan will be one man," to which the other replied, "Farquhar will be two." On hearing this, the man, who had been so securely tied, sprang to his feet, broke his bonds like spider threads, jumped overboard, and made off with the two friends, who had been coming to his rescue.

FAIRY SUPERSTITIONS

In old Scotland, the *Northern Lights* were thought of as fallen angels fighting everlasting battles. The red cloud that appears below the lights is a pool of their blood. When the blood falls to Earth, it congeals into rocks called "blood stones." These stones are known in the Hebrides (western isles of Scotland) as Elf's blood.

THE MERMAID AND MERMAN

The Mermaid of the Scottish Highlands was the same as in the rest of the kingdom: a sea creature, half fish and half woman, with long, dishevelled hair, which she combs at night while sitting on the rocks by the shore. She has been known to cast off the fishy covering of her lower limbs. Anyone who finds it can, by hiding it, detain her from ever returning to the sea again. There is a common story in the Highlands, and also in Ireland, that a person so detained her for years, married her, and had a family by her. One of the family fell in with the covering, and telling his mother of the pretty thing he had found, she recovered possession of it and escaped to the sea. She pursues ships and is dangerous. Sailors throw empty barrels overboard, and while she spends her time examining the barrels, the sailors make their escape.

A man in Skye caught a Mermaid and kept her for a year. She gave him much curious information. When parting, he asked her what virtue or evil there was in egg water (water in which eggs had been boiled). She said, "If I tell you that, you will have a tale to tell," and disappeared.

A native of *Eilein Anabuich* (the "Unripe Island"), a village in North Harris, caught a Mermaid on a rock, and to procure her release, she granted him three wishes. He became a skillful herb doctor, who could cure the king's evil and other diseases ordinarily incurable; he became a prophet, who could foretell, particularly to women, whatever was to befall people; and he obtained a remarkably fine voice. This latter gift he had only had before in his own estimation; when he sang, others did not think his voice fine or even tolerable.

The Havfrue, or Mermaid, is represented in the popular tradition sometimes as good and at other times evil and treacherous. She is

A Mermaid looking upon the shore for her snow-white cattle.

beautiful in her appearance. Fishermen sometimes see her in the bright summer's sun, when a thin mist hangs over the sea, sitting on the surface of the water, combing her long, golden hair with a golden comb or driving up her snow-white cattle to feed on the strands and small islands.

MERMAID-TRACKING TIP

Lighting a fire near the ocean can sometimes draw a cold Mermaid out of the water for warmth.

At other times, she comes as a beautiful maiden, chilled and shivering with the cold of the night, to the fires the fishers have kindled, hoping by this means to entice them to her love. Her appearance prognosticates both storm and ill success in their fishing. People who are drowned and whose bodies are not found are believed to be taken into the dwellings of the Mermaids.

Mermaids are also supposed to have the power of foretelling future events. In all countries, fortune-telling has been a gift of the sea people.

The Merman is described as of a handsome form, with green or black hair and beard. He dwells either in the bottom of the sea or in the cliffs and hills near the seashore, and is regarded as rather a good and beneficent kind of being.

THE WATER-HORSE

The belief in the existence of the Water-horse is now generally a thing of the past in the Highlands, but in olden times almost every lonely freshwater lake was tenanted by one, sometimes by several, of these animals. In shape and colour, it resembled an ordinary horse and was often mistaken for one. It was seen passing from one lake to another, mixing with the farmers' horses in the adjoining pastures, and it waylaid belated travellers who passed near its haunts. It was highly dangerous to touch or mount a Water-horse. Those whom it decoyed into doing so were taken away to the loch in which it had its haunt and were there devoured. It was said to make its approaches also in other guises—as a young man, a boy, a ring, and even a tuft of wool; any woman upon whom it set its mark was certain to become its victim. A cow-shackle around its neck or a cap on its head completely subdued it, and as long as either of these was kept on it, it could be as safely employed in farm labour as any other horse.

A Water-horse portrayed in both its horse and human form.

In Skye, it was said to have a sharp bill (*gob biorach*) or, as others describe it, a narrow, slippery, brown snout. Accounts agree that it had a long, flowing tail and mane.

In colour, it was sometimes grey, sometimes black, and sometimes black with a white spot on its forehead. This variation arose, some say, from the Water-horse being of any colour, like other horses, and others say it comes from its having the power of changing its colour as well as its shape. When it came in the shape of a human, it was detected by its horse-hoofs and by the green water weeds or sand in its hair. It was then very amorous, but it was the end of those who were unfortunate enough to encounter it, to then be taken to the loch and devoured. Whatever benefit the farmer might at first derive from securing one with the cap or cow-shackle, the farmer would soon be met with ruinous loss.

The following tales will illustrate the character of the superstition better than a lengthened dissertation.

Cru-loch is a lonely little lake above Ardachyle (the height of the sound) in the north-east of Mull. A person passing it late at night, on his way home, saw a horse with a saddle on, quietly feeding at the loch side. He went toward it with the intention of riding it home, but in time he observed green-water herbs about its feet and refrained from touching it. He walked on and, before long, was overtaken by a stranger, who said that unless he (the Water-horse, who was also the speaker) had been friendly and a well-wisher, he would have taken the man to the loch. Among other supernatural information, it told the man the day of his death.

Another tale takes place on the Isle of Coll. At noontide, while the cattle were standing in the loch, the herdsman near Loch Annla was visited by a person in whose head he observed *rathum*, that is, water weeds. When going away, the stranger jumped into the loch and disappeared without doing any harm. People used to hear strange noises about that loch, no doubt caused by the Water-horse, which was the herdsman's visitor.

THE KELPIE

The Kelpie that swells torrents and devours women and children has no representative in Gaelic superstition. Some writers speak as if the Water-horse were to be identified with it, but the two animals are distinctly separate. The Water-horse haunts lochs, the Kelpie streams and torrents. The former is never accused of swelling torrents any more than of causing any other natural phenomenon, nor of taking away children, unless perhaps when wanting to silence a refractory child.

A Shetland friend writes: "Kelpies, I cannot remember of ever hearing what shape they were of. They generally did their mischief in a quiet way, such as being seen splashing the water about the burns, and taking hold of the water-wheel of mills and holding them still. I have heard a man declare that his mill was stopped one night for half an hour and the full power of water on the wheel, and he was frightened himself to go out and see what was wrong. And he not only said but maintained that it was a Kelpie or something of that kind that did it."

The Kelpie is said to reside near streams and torrents.

THE WATER-BULL

This animal, unlike the Water-horse, was of harmless character and did no mischief to those who came near its haunts. It stayed in little lonely moorland lochs, whence it issued only at night. It was then heard lowing near the loch, and it came among the farmers' cattle but was seldom seen. Calves having short ears, as if the upper part had been cut off with a knife or, as it is termed in Gaelic, *Carc-chluasach* ("knife-eared"), were said to be its offspring. It had no ears itself, and hence its calves had only half ears.

A Water-bull's short ears are one way to distinguish it from bulls with no connection to the supernatural realm.

In the district of Lorn, a dairy-maid and herder, before leaving the fold in the evening in which the cows had been gathered to be milked, saw a small, ugly, very black animal, bull-shaped, soft and slippery, coming among the herd. It had an unnatural bellow, something like the crowing of a cock. The man and woman fled in terror but, on coming back in the morning, found the cattle lying in the fold as though nothing had occurred.

THE KING OTTER

The Water-dog (*Dobhar-Chù*), also called the King Otter (*Righ nan Dòbhran*), is a formidable animal, seldom seen, having a skin of magic power that is worth as many guineas as are required to cover it. It goes at the head of every band of seven, some say nine, otters, and is never killed without the death of a man, woman, or dog. It has a white spot below the chin, on which alone it is vulnerable. A piece of its skin keeps misfortune away from the house in which it is kept, renders the soldier invulnerable in battle by arrow or sword or bullet, and, placed in the banner, makes the enemy turn and fly. "An inch of it placed on the soldier's eye," as a Lochaber informant said, "kept him from harm or hurt or wound though bullets flew about him like hailstones and naked swords clashed at his breast. When a direct aim was taken, the gun refused fire."

Others say the vulnerable white spot was under the King Otter's arm and no larger than a sixpence. When the hunter took aim, he needed to hit this precise spot, or else he fell a prey to the animal's dreadful jaws. In Raasa and the opposite mainland, the magic power was said to be in a jewel in its head, which made its possessor invulnerable and secured the person good

A King Otter with a jewel-shaped marking on its head.

fortune; in other respects, the belief regarding the King Otter is the same as elsewhere.

The word *dobhar* (pronounced "dooar" or "dour"), signifying water, is obsolete in Gaelic except in the name of this animal.

BIASD NA SROGAIG

This mythical animal, "the beast of the lowering horn," seems to have been peculiar to Skye. It had but one horn on its forehead and, like the Water-bull, stayed in lochs. It was a large animal with long legs, of a clumsy and inelegant make, not heavy and thick but tall and awkward. Its principal use seems to have been to keep children quiet, and it would be no wonder if, in the majority of cases, the terrors of childhood became a creed in later years. *Scrogag*, from which it derives its name, is a ludicrous name given to a snuff horn and refers to the solitary horn on its forehead.

The Biasd Na Srogaig *is an awkward-looking long-legged unicorn that lives in or near a lake.*

THE BIG BEAST OF LOCHAWE

This animal (*Beathach mòr Loch Odha*) had twelve legs and was to be heard in wintertime, breaking the ice. Some say it was like a horse; others, like a large eel.

147

MORE MAGICAL CREATURES FROM SCANDINAVIA

Scandinavia includes the kingdoms of Sweden, Denmark, and Norway, which once had a common religion and a common language. Scandinavian mythology was built on a belief that the whole world was filled with spirits of various kinds. These were divided into the Celestial and the Terrestrial from their places of abode. The former were, according to the ideas of those times, of a good and elevated nature, and of a friendly disposition toward men, whence they also received the name of White or Light Elves or Spirits. The latter, on the contrary, who were classified after their abodes in air, sea, and earth, were not regarded in so favourable a light.

ELVES

Say, knowest thou the Elves' gay and joyous race?
The banks of streams are their home;
They spin of the moonshine their holiday-dress,
With their lily-white hands frolicsome.

A good Elf curled inside a berry bush to sleep.

While the Elf of the British Isles was one and the same as a Fairy, the Scandinavian Elf had its own unique identity.

The Alfar, as their Elf is called, still lives in the memory and traditions of Scandinavians. They also, to a certain extent, retain their distinction as White or Black. The former, or the Good Elves, dwell in the air, dance on the grass, or sit in the leaves of trees; the latter, or the Evil Elves, are regarded as an underground people who frequently inflict sickness or injury on mankind; for which there is a particular kind of doctor, called Kloka män, to be met with in all parts of Scandinavia.

ELF-TRACKING TIP

If you're looking for a good and benevolent Elf, look up. Elves tend to live above ground and high in trees. If you see an Elf coming up out of the ground or out from under someone's home, steer clear. It is likely to be an evil Elf or at least a terribly mischievous one.

The Elves are believed to have their kings and to celebrate their weddings and banquets, just the same as the dwellers above ground. There is an interesting intermediate class of Elves in popular tradition called the Hill-people (*Högfolk*), who are believed to dwell in caves and small hills; when they show themselves, they have an attractive human form. The common people seem to connect with them a deep feeling of melancholy, as if bewailing a half-quenched hope of redemption.

People cannot tell much more about them besides their sweet singing, which may occasionally, on summer nights, be heard out of their hills. One may stand still and listen, or, as it is expressed in the ballads, "lays their ear to the Elve-hill," but no one must be so cruel as, by the slightest word, to destroy their hopes of salvation, for then the spritely music will be turned into weeping and lamentation.

The Norwegians call the Elves *Huldrafolk*, and their music Huldraslaat; it is in the minor key and of a dull and mournful sound. The mountaineers sometimes play it and pretend they have learned it by listening to the underground people among the hills and rocks. There is also a tune called the Elf-king's tune, which several of the good fiddlers know right well but never venture to play, for as soon as it begins, both old and young, and even inanimate objects, are impelled to dance, and the player cannot stop unless he can play the air backward or someone comes behind him and cuts the strings of his fiddle.

A bad Elf emerging from its underground abode is best avoided.

At one time, it is said, a servant girl was greatly beloved by the Elves for her clean, tidy habits, particularly because she was careful to carry away all dirt and foul water to a distance from the house. The Elves invited her to a wedding. Everything was conducted in the greatest order, and they made her a present of some chips, which she took good-humouredly and put into her pocket. But when the bride-pair was coming, there was a straw unluckily lying in the way. The bridegroom got cleverly over it, but the poor bride fell on her face. At the sight of this, the girl could not restrain herself and burst out a-laughing, and at that instant, the whole vanished from her sight. The next day, to her utter amazement, she found that what she had taken to be nothing but chips were so many pieces of pure gold.

The Elves are extremely fond of dancing in the meadows, where they form circles of a livelier green that are called Elf-dance (*Elfdans*). When the country people see stripes along the dewy grass in the woods and meadows in the morning, they say the Elves have been dancing there. If anyone should, at midnight, get within their circle, they become visible to that person but then may elude the person. Not everyone can see the Elves; one person may see them dancing while another perceives nothing. The Elves, however, have the power to bestow this gift on whomsoever they please. People also used to speak of Elf-books, which Elves gave to those whom they loved and which enabled them to foretell future events.

The Elves often sit in little stones that are of a circular form and are called Elf-mills (*Elf-quärnor*); the sound of their voices is said to be sweet and soft like the air.

In the popular creed, there is some strange connection between the Elves and the trees. They not only frequent them, but they

Mermaids, Water-horses, and Kelpies

Dwarfs

Elves

Fairies

A map featuring the various terrains where magical creatures reside.

make an interchange of form with them. In the churchyard of Store Heddinge, in Zealand, there are the remains of an oak tree. These, say the common people, are the Elle-king's soldiers: by day, they are trees; by night, valiant warriors. In the wood of Rugaard, on the same island, is a tree that by night becomes a whole Elle-people and goes about all alive. It has no leaves upon it, yet it would be very unsafe to go to break or fell it, for the underground people frequently hold their meetings under its branches.

MAGICAL-BEING SUPERSTITIONS

Sunday children, as they are called (those born on a Sunday), are remarkable for possessing the property of seeing Elves and similar beings.

DWARFS

The Dwarfs, or Hill (Berg) Trolls, were appointed the hills; the Elves, the groves and leafy trees; the Hill-people (*Högfolk*), the caves and caverns; the Mermen, Mermaids, and Necks, the sea, lakes, and rivers; the River-man (*Strömkarl*) the small waterfalls. Both the Catholic and Protestant clergy have endeavoured to excite an aversion to these beings, but in vain. They are regarded as possessing considerable power over man and nature, and it is believed that though now unhappy, they will be eventually saved, or *faa förlossning* ("get salvation"), as it is expressed.

A band of merry Dwarfs.

We now return to the Baltic, to the Isle of Rügen. The inhabitants of Rügen believe in three kinds of Dwarfs, or underground people: the White, the Brown, and the Black, so named from the colour of their garments and apparatus.

The White are the most delicate of all and are of an innocent and gentle disposition. During the winter, when the face of nature is cold, raw, and cheerless, they remain still and quiet in their hills, solely engaged in the fashioning of the finest works in silver and gold, of too delicate a texture for mortal eyes to discern. Thus they pass the winter, but no sooner does the spring return than they abandon their recesses and live through all the summer above ground, in sunshine and starlight, in uninterrupted revelry and enjoyment. The moment the trees and flowers begin to sprout and bud in the early days of spring, they emerge from their hills and get among the stalks and branches, and thence to the blossoms and flowers, where they sit and gaze around them. In the night, when mortals sleep, the White

Dwarfs come forth and dance their joyous rounds in the green grass, about the hills, brooks, and springs, making the sweetest and most delicate music, which bewilders travellers, who hear and wonder at the strains of the invisible musicians. They may, if they will, go out by day, but never in company; these daylight rambles are allowed them only when alone and under some assumed form. They therefore frequently fly about in the shape of parti-coloured little birds or butterflies, or snow-white doves, showing kindness and benevolence to the good who merit their favour.

Fig. 7

Fig. 6

Fig. 5

There are notable differences between the temperaments of a White (Figure 5), Brown (Figure 6), and Black Dwarf (Figure 7).

Birds, butterflies, and white doves, when seen in the daytime, may be the chosen form of a White Dwarf who has decided to come out during the day.

The Brown Dwarfs are less than eighteen inches high. They wear little brown coats and jackets and brown caps with little silver bells on them. Some of them wear black shoes with red strings in them. In general, however, they wear fine glass shoes; at their dances, none of them wear any other. They are very handsome, with clear, light-coloured eyes and small, most beautiful hands and feet. They on the whole have cheerful, good-natured dispositions, mingled with some roguish traits. Like the White Dwarfs, they are great artists in gold and silver, working so curiously as to astonish those who happen to see their performances. At night, they come out of their hills and dance by the light of the moon and stars. They also glide invisibly into people's houses, their caps rendering them imperceptible by all who do not have similar caps. They possess an unlimited power of transformation and can pass through the smallest keyholes. Frequently, they bring with them presents for children, or they lay gold rings, ducats, and the like in their way, and often are invisibly present to save children from the perils of fire and water. They plague and annoy lazy servants and untidy maids with frightful dreams; oppress them with nightmares; bite them like fleas; and scratch and tear them like cats and dogs. Often, in the night, Brown Dwarfs take the shape of owls, thieves, and lovers to frighten these people, or, like will-o'-the-wisps, lead them astray into bogs and marshes or perhaps to those who are in pursuit of them.

The Black Dwarfs wear black jackets and caps and are not handsome like the others. On the contrary, they are ugly, with weeping eyes, like those of blacksmiths and colliers. They are the most expert workers, especially in steel, to which they can give a degree at once of hardness and flexibility that no human smith can imitate; the swords they make will bend like rushes and are as hard as diamonds. In old times, arms and armour made by Black Dwarfs were in great demand; shirts of mail manufactured by them were as fine as cobwebs, yet no bullet would penetrate them, and no helm or corslet could resist the swords they fashioned, but all these things have now gone out of use.

These Dwarfs are of malicious, ill dispositions, and they delight in doing mischief to humankind. They are unsocial, and there are seldom more than two or three of them seen together; they keep mostly in their hills and seldom come out in the daytime, nor do they ever go far from home. People say that in the summer, they are fond of sitting under the elder-trees, the smell of which is very pleasing to them, and that anyone who wants anything of them must go there and call them.

Some say they have no music and dancing, only howling and whimpering. When a screaming is heard in the woods and marshes, like that of crying children, or a mewing and screeching, like that of a multitude of cats or owls, the sounds just might be made by the vociferous Dwarfs.

THE NECK

The Neck (in Danish, *Nökke*) is the river-spirit. The ideas surrounding him are various. Sometimes, he is represented as sitting on the surface of the water on summer nights, resembling a little boy with golden hair hanging in ringlets and a red cap on his head. Sometimes he appears above the water like a handsome young man, but beneath the water like a horse; at other times, as an old man with a long beard out of which he wrings the water as he sits on the cliffs. In this last form, Odin, according to the Icelandic sagas, has sometimes revealed himself.

A Neck (river-spirit) playing his harp while sitting by the river at sunset.

The Neck is very severe against any haughty maiden who makes an ill return to the love of her wooer, but should he himself fall in love with a maid of human kind, he is the most polite and attentive suitor in the world.

He sits on the water and plays on his gold harp, the harmony of which operates on all nature. To hear his music, a person must present him with a black lamb and also promise him resurrection and redemption.

With the knowledge of Fairies and other magical beings that you now possess, having uncovered a treasury of mystical folklore of the fantastic creatures that were once understood to live among us, it is up to you, dear modern reader, to venture out at your own risk into nature and determine your own beliefs. May you be blessed with many incredible encounters, may your eyes and ears be tuned to what lies beyond the framework of science, and may you succeed in restoring that child-like sense of wonder that revels in myth and mystery.